Copyright © 2021 by Reena Gupta
All rights reserved.

Wisdocity Publications
www.careerinterrupted.net

BOOK DESIGN BY Ivica Jandrijević
JACKET DESIGN BY Peter Sucheski
ILLUSTRATIONS BY Elena Brighittini
DEVELOPMENT EDITING BY Dan Crissman
STRUCTURE, PROOFREADING BY Ritika Gupta

ISBN:
978-1-955450-00-3 (HARDBACK)
978-1-955450-01-0 (PAPERBACK)
978-1-955450-02-7 (EBOOK)

No part of this publication may be reproduced or transmitted in any form or by any means, electronic or mechanical, including photocopy, recording or any information storage and retrieval system, without permission in writing from the copyright owners. Every reasonable attempt has been made to identify owners of copyright. Any errors or omissions brought to the publisher's attention will be corrected in subsequent editions.

CAREER INTERRUPTED

REENA GUPTA
with Rebecca Cullen

WISDOCITY PUBLICATIONS

TABLE OF CONTENTS

FOREWORD 1

PROLOGUE 3

INTRODUCTION 7

ABOUT THE AUTHORS 11

    Reena Gupta 11

    Rebecca Cullen 13

    Our Book Village 15

PART ONE

REALIZE

WHO ARE YOU AND HOW YOU GOT HERE

ONE DOOR CLOSES 37

CONSCIOUSLY UNCOUPLING FROM YOUR CAREER 43

PARENTAL INDECISION 51

GETTING BACK IN THE GAME 59

GET YOUR STORY STRAIGHT 67

CORE COMPETENCIES 77

ALIGNMENT FRAMEWORK 83

SUCCESS VS. HAPPINESS 93

BALANCING YOUR THREE-LEGGED STOOL 103

CHECKLIST 117

PART TWO

REINVEST

PREPARE YOURSELF

LIFELONG LEARNING... 121

MENTOR, COACH, GURU, GUIDE............................. 129

HOW TO NETWORK EFFECTIVELY............................ 139

FIND YOUR PROFESSIONAL ECOSYSTEM 149

YOU AS A BRAND... 159

BODY, MIND AND SOUL WELLNESS 167

FAMILY, FRIENDS AND YOUR SUPPORT SYSTEM............... 181

CHECKLIST 191

PART THREE

RELAUNCH

HOW TO BE WHAT YOU WANT TO BE

CHOOSE YOUR PATH TO SUCCESS 195

HOW TO PULL OFF A SUCCESSFUL CAREER CHANGE 209

SO, YOU WANT TO BE AN ENTREPRENEUR.................... 215

REACH YOUR POTENTIAL IN A TRADITIONAL JOB............ 241

SUCCEED AS YOUR OWN ONE PERSON ARMY 255

YOUR CANVAS 275

EPILOGUE 281

ACKNOWLEDGMENTS 285

*This book is dedicated to
my friend, my mentor, my Dad,*
Narmdeshwar Nath Gupta

*He taught me the three most important life skills:
will power, help others, keep smiling*

FOREWORD

I HAVE GREAT ADMIRATION and respect for Reena Gupta and her ambitious mission of guiding people to find that ever-elusive balance in their personal and professional lives with *Career Interrupted*.

As I have discussed in my teachings and in my books, we live in an intensely disruptive and interesting moment in time. What is so badly needed, and what Reena offers with this book, is not simply a generic career guide, but rather an urging to take a 30,000-foot view. Think about what you want for your life, and then mold your career to that. So many do the reverse, making work a priority and wondering why they feel so empty inside. It has sadly become the way for so many people around the globe.

I lost my lovely wife, Tavinder, too soon, but she understood that if your idea of success is earning more and more money, you've missed the point of life. My wife put her hopes and ambitions aside to see me succeed and to raise our children, and she was just coming into her own professionally when she tragically became ill. If there is any lesson she taught me, it's that you have to look into your heart and always listen to what your heart wants. If your life is out of balance and you know more about the inner lives of your colleagues than your own friends and family, something is out of whack.

What I love about this book is that the message of inclusion resonates so strongly with the work I have done raising awareness about the racism and gender gap that exists in this country, particularly in tech, in Silicon Valley. You will come up against obstacles and you will often be told "can't," but you must always believe in your own talent, lean into your strengths, and with hope and resilience, knock down all those roadblocks that stand in your way.

This is not a superficial book—it is highly personalized. Reena is urging the reader to take a deep dive and use a holistic approach to connect with what makes you tick, and to discover your secret formula to success. This will be different for each of us. I really like her concept of developing that awareness and building a framework to be truly in touch with your innermost hopes, fears, and motivations, and start crafting a career path where you can be of service to yourself and others.

In *Career Interrupted* Reena makes it clear that networking and mentoring is not a transactional relationship—there is a give and take. If we continually pay our knowledge and our good luck forward, we can bring humanity back to the corporate world and create a more inclusive work culture.

This book should be taught alongside celebrated books about success, economics, and marketing. Anyone searching for meaning in their personal and professional life will benefit from knowing that when you plumb your deeper self to get in touch with who you are, who you used to be, and who you want to be, you will begin to achieve clarity. When you become strategic and act with intention, you will find you are the one in control, steering your own ship and blazing a trail to success. Bravo *Career Interrupted* for being the guide to lead you on that most personal sojourn.

~ Vivek Wadhwa

Distinguished Fellow at Harvard Law School. Vivek has written several acclaimed books, including *Innovating Women: The Changing Face of Technology*. He has been a globally syndicated columnist for *The Washington Post* and held appointments at Duke University and Stanford Law School, and he has been named one of *Time* magazine's 40 most influential minds in technology.

PROLOGUE

AFTER MY SON was born, I was lying in bed, plagued by intermittent fever and inexplicable virus-like symptoms for months. We had just moved into our starter home in Nashville. My husband, Rajeev, earned a decent living as a software engineer for GE. So, from a financial standpoint, it would be fine if I took a career break, dealt with the confounding, stressful health issues, and stayed home to raise my child.

It was 2002, a dozen years before Sheryl Sandberg's book was published. Back then if you said the words, "Lean In," people would have thought you were hard of hearing. Few people understood my passion for work. Some relatives even made it seem as though I had to choose between a career and a happy family life. I knew in my heart that this was not the case. I chose to keep working.

In the months after my son, Rohan, was born none of the doctors I went to could explain my malaise. After announcing my decision to return to work, my mother, back in India, fretted. She let me know that my counterintuitive, salmon-swimming-upstream inclination was not the right choice. Nevertheless, the next Monday morning, feeling lousy and combating a low-grade fever, I put on my favorite power suit, got in my 1997 Nissan Sentra, and went back to work. It was a decision my family and I never looked back on.

When I reflect on the way my own story unfolded, I find that there is so much I want to say about how people develop professionally—how we find ourselves and shape our futures by leveraging the real combination of our drive, our circumstances, and the opportunities we create. I took some time to deliberately examine all the pivotal moments in my own career—how my life decisions shaped my career path, and vice-versa. The first seed for writing this book was planted. But I wanted to write a book that would do more than just inspire and teach. I wanted to write a book that would open up conversations about career and the elusive work-life balance we're all chasing.

Fortuitously, Rebecca, my writing partner, turned out to be the perfect person to write this book with me. While I returned to work right after having my first child, Rebecca took a career break. Like many people who become the cheerleader in their spouse's career, Rebecca felt like she stepped out so long that she lost her mojo, and that her professional identity was in crisis. While she is incredibly proud of the two very dynamic, creative, and compassionate boys she raised while she was a stay-at-home mom, she knows that if she had to do it over again a healthy work-life balance would have been much better for her emotional, spiritual, and professional development.

I was somehow able to manage a work-life balance, which I defined more as work-life harmony. My children, Ritika, fourteen, and

Rohan, nineteen have grown into very loving, thoughtful kids, both of whom give expression to the family's trademark entrepreneurial genes! I am often asked how I manage to do all that I am doing professionally, still manage to focus on my family, *and* maintain my own sanity and well-being. I have a lot to say on that subject.

I still haven't met Superwoman, not even in the mirror I check before I leave the house. I would never say it's been a breeze. But dealing with challenges as they came up over the nineteen years that span my career I developed a greater understanding for what working people raising a family deal with every day.

I reminisced. I watered that first writing-a-book seed.

I am proud of these nineteen years, I'm proud of my career and the fruit of its issue—developing software, founding multiple companies including Avankia, TargetRecruit, Mom Relaunch, and now Career Interrupted, and coaching people at all junctures of their career paths. The first person I ever hired was a stay-at-home mom. This was in 2003. She was worried that her resume was unimpressive, but I knew her well. I knew her strengths and I was convinced that given an opportunity and a little coaching she would do a great job. Seeing her thrive was an incentive for me to continue the work of nurturing less-obvious candidates—whether they were moms returning to the workforce, immigrants with no networking connections, or any number of disenfranchised groups.

When I reached out to Rebecca, we talked about my mission of nurturing people going through a career transition and decided that we wanted to harness that power and put it in a book. I wanted these ideas to reach a larger audience and impact as many lives as possible with a positive, uplifting message of what can be possible when you re-imagine life. Rebecca and I started outlining the book. The seed sprouts.

We began collaborating in early 2020. Suddenly the ground beneath all of our feet shifted. I will be forgiven for saying it shifted quite dramatically. A new pandemic, caused by a novel coronavirus, began to upend, and interrupt, careers on a global scale. This is not hyperbole. Rebecca and I spied an opportunity to help people affected by the sudden disruption of furloughs and layoffs, to help anyone who stepped out to take a career break, to help anyone who is burnt out, in a career rut, or transitioning back to work after a break.

We acknowledge that over the last few decades, some great books came before ours, and we knew that in order to create a powerful career guide we would have to reach people on a gut level. With inspirations like *What Color Is Your Parachute* and *Forever Employable*, we aimed high by aspiring to sit on the shelf next to these classics. Let this book be your North Star, guiding you on a path to leading your best personal and professional life.

INTRODUCTION

THERE ARE SO many disruptors in life—external disruptors like global health crises or massive shifts in technology that level entire industries—and then there are internal disruptors, like personal crises or life changes that create a fork in your professional road. Almost all of us have found ourselves at a career crossroads at some point in our lives. Every career interruption, whether it is your choice or someone else's, comes with its own set of issues.

If you're leaving the workforce, you may worry—are my accomplishments and skills going to become irrelevant? Will I lose my mojo? Will I lose my identity? It can be intimidating when you're just re-entering the workforce. You may wonder: Did I step out so long that I've become completely replaceable? Am I out of touch with the breakneck pace of technology? Are my skills obsolete?

A layoff or a furlough can be a huge blow to your ego. While these are generally impersonal affairs, it can *feel* extremely personal, and it can also be very scary. It's not just career uncertainty you're dealing with, now you're dealing with financial insecurity as well. You're navigating so much while managing to keep your morale up, and trying to remain optimistic in these new, uncharted waters.

The purpose of this book is to be your mentor, guru, and guide through all these turbulent waters and troubled times. We're going to get you to the other side. We are very excited to have worked out, via our Tri-R Methodology, an actionable strategy that does just that.

The book is broken down into sections that correlate to the three Rs of the Tri-R Methodology: Realize, Reinvest, Relaunch. And though each chapter has value as a stand-alone chapter, if you read the book straight through, there is a layering process that I will liken to baking an amazing lasagna. You start with fresh, quality ingredients. On their own, each of the ingredients is pretty tasty. But skillfully layering them and then baking the dish allows them to blend in such a way that when it's done, the flavors are in full bloom and the whole is much more impactful than its parts.

In the first section, Realize, you will assess where you are professionally and emotionally. You will get clear on your core competencies, values, and what happiness would look and feel like for you. Most importantly, we start you down the road of achieving work-life harmony.

The second section, Reinvest, takes an actionable approach to having you up your game. You're going to learn how to seek out mentors, hone your personal brand, and network in addition to focusing on your own wellness.

In the third section, Relaunch, we take a close look at what entrepreneurial, traditional, and freelance career paths look like, and you will learn what it takes to find work-life harmony, no matter which path you choose.

We don't want you to get the wrong impression. This is not merely a how-to, self-help guide. What we are offering is a means for everyone who picks up this book to personalize their quest by doing a deep-dive assessment—where they are coming from, how they got here, what matters to them, what they are good at—and then connecting these deep values and core competencies to a career path that will be fulfilling, both personally and financially.

At the heart of the Tri-R Methodology is work-life harmony, symbolized by the three-legged stool. If you hold a vision of a three-legged stool with one leg being your career, one leg being friends and family, and one leg being wellness, it creates a framework that you can visualize and continually check in with. If your stool becomes unbalanced, you know you need to make adjustments.

At the end of the book, we've created a cutting-edge, practical toolkit which is the Tri-R Canvas—a visual chart with elements you will fill in using the thought-provoking questions at the end of each chapter that are intended to help you delve deeper into the topic. Ultimately, your canvas will serve as a blueprint to inspire and motivate you going forward in whatever career path you choose. Please download the online version of the workbook at Career Interrupted[1]. Create a copy to use as you read the book.

This book is full of wisdom supplied by people from diverse backgrounds. We wanted to comprehensively address the world of work from every perspective, and we were lucky enough to procure compelling interviews from people who either took a career break, re-entered the workforce after a career break, or who experienced career burnout or parental indecision, as well as from supporting players who helped their partners segue back into the workforce. We also spoke with professors, authors, technopreneurs, and various experts in the fields of business, human resources, talent, online learning, positive psychology, and entrepreneurialism. Prior to writing this book, we honestly had no idea that there was such a thing as a motherhood clarity mentor, but we found an excellent

---

1   www.careerinterrupted.net

motherhood clarity mentor who is the top in her field! Combining our research and expertise and incorporating the shared experience of these diverse experts across so many disciplines put the "meat on the bones" that gives this book the power to truly change people's lives.

One of the themes woven throughout the book echoes the proverb, "A rising tide lifts all boats." The idea that when we help each other we help ourselves is the way I was raised, and it provided the impetus for me to found Mom Relaunch.

Whatever your journey has been so far, and wherever you wind up, *Career Interrupted* will serve as a road map that guides you through this challenging juncture and gets you on a path to achieve your own work-life harmony.

ABOUT THE AUTHORS

Reena Gupta

When I moved to the US from India, my husband, Rajeev, and I first settled in Nashville, where I started out as an independent consultant before moving on to create an IT staffing and consulting company. I also founded a software company called TargetRecruit, an applicant tracking system for staffing companies. My current passions are the two companies I founded—*Mom Relaunch* and *Career Interrupted,* both of which nurture and mentor a goldmine of hidden talent like stay-at-home parents, and people from all walks of life who are at their career crossroads for whatever reason.

I advocate for diversity and inclusion, reaching out to companies looking for talent who share the same vision.

I am living proof that a small-town girl from India can become a successful solo bootstrapped entrepreneur despite not having a business background, advanced business degrees, or connections. With a story of how tenacity and perseverance can create a fulfilled, regret-free, and harmonious life I hope to do my part to nurture others to live to their highest potential. And because I see work-life harmony as a combination of all aspects of living, I am sharing a few personal details to round out my bio.

Mentoring is a theme throughout this book. I was blessed to have incredible mentors at every stage in my career, and I try to pay that forward, coaching and encouraging the next generation. I have gotten passionately involved in my community and I have a hard time saying no—whether it's teaching courses on entrepreneurship, organizing events, or taking on a cause that needs attention. My greatest joy is my family and friends. I enjoy the quiet of small moments, but I love big adventures as well. I have traveled the world, and I've visited all fifty states in the U.S. I try to celebrate New Year's Eve in a different country every year.

Rebecca Cullen

After having my son, Aidan, and then three years later his little brother, Beckett, I stepped away from a promising career in screenwriting, stayed home to raise the kids and was a supporting player in my ex-husband's career. Since our separation, I've been chosen as one of 20 finalists out of 2,000 submissions for an HBO diversity fellowship, I have published work in the LA Times, published a book, optioned a screenplay, and fully relaunched myself, with the help of my fantastic village (including my agent and manager!)

Reena somehow found me online, and the phrase, "You complete me," from *Jerry Maguire* comes to mind. We fell in step right from the start—our strengths and talents forming a perfect yin and yang for three reasons. The first was the benefit of writing this book from two divergent backgrounds: the ambitious entrepreneur who went back to work two months after her first child was born, and the stay-at-home parent who stepped out of her career for a dozen years. The second part of our magical formula was the complementary talents that we bring to the table. Reena has an incredibly impressive background of knowledge in the talent industry; I have my writing skills. Thirdly, there was a soul-sister bond that formed which neither of us had anticipated from her randomly finding me on LinkedIn.

It's partly an East meets West sharing of ideas and learning from each other, accidentally becoming key support players in each other's lives as we delved deeper into what we wanted to say, tossing out the original outline and carving out a path together with a much deeper, stronger message.

We hope the passion that we both share for empowering each and every person to find their calling and live a rich and rewarding life resonates with anyone who feels disenfranchised, left behind, or at a career crossroads in their life. Our mission is to pass on the experience of work-life harmony we both shared writing this book together.

Our Book Village

In *Career Interrupted* there is a lot of talk about finding your village, and the critical importance of support, mentoring, and contribution from those close to you to help you shine. And this book could not have been realized without the meaningful contribution of those who have been kind enough to give their time and share their expertise in these pages. Having broken the larger topics into subtopics, we were able to attract dynamic and interesting interviews for every niche that add a layer of depth to the themes awash in the undercurrent of the book. Everyone we have included has helped illuminate specific points in each chapter, and together, we've woven a tapestry that we think both highlights larger themes and pulls our message together—empowerment through creating work-life harmony.

Ann Davidman (pages 52, 53, 54)

Ann Davidman, Marriage & Family Therapist, Parenthood Clarity Mentor, and author, uses mindful decision-making to help women and men make one of the most important choices in their lifetime. Ann believes every person has the right to explore their own truthful answer to the question, Is parenthood for me? This has been her passion for thirty years. Ann offers online clarity courses for women and men. www.IsParenthoodForMe.com.

Anuradha Basu (pages 221, 222)

Dr. Anuradha Basu is Professor of Entrepreneurship in the Lucas College & Graduate School of Business, and Director of the Silicon Valley Center for Entrepreneurship at San Jose State University (SJSU). Her research interests include immigrant, minority, and transnational entrepreneurs, and entrepreneurship education. She has advised numerous aspiring entrepreneurs and is Faculty Advisor to the IDEAS Club at SJSU. She earned a PhD in Economics from the University of Cambridge, UK.

Ashley Connell (pages 55, 56, 57, 89, 170)

Ashley Connell, CEO and Founder of Prowess, is one-part fearless entrepreneur, one-part fearless women's advocate. For the first fifteen years of her career, she was an award-winning tech marketer in both Austin and London. Ashley's unstoppable drive to have both a career and time for family motivated her to start Prowess. Her commitment to changing the lives of overloaded employers, women seeking rewarding work, and those affected by the gender pay gap, has landed her thought leadership pieces in Forbes, Built in Austin and at SXSW. In her pretty much non-existent spare time she enjoys yoga, spaghetti and meatballs, walks with her bulldog, and cheering on her beloved Longhorns.

Avanish Sahai (pages 149, 154, 155, 156)

Avanish is an India-born, Brazil-raised, US-educated senior technology executive, investor, and entrepreneur. He is head of the global technology partner ecosystem for Google Cloud; has held leadership roles at companies such as Oracle, McKinsey, Salesforce, and ServiceNow and was a C-level executive at venture-backed companies. He is also an angel investor, and serves on the Board of Hubspot (NYSE:HUBS). He holds an MBA from UCLA Anderson, an MS in Computer Engineering from Boston University, and a BS in Electronic Engineering from the University of São Paulo, Brazil.

ABOUT THE AUTHORS

Barry Asin (pages 256, 261, 262)

A leading authority on workforce solutions worldwide, Barry Asin is renowned for his expertise on staffing and contingent labor. President of Staffing Industry Analysts (SIA) since 2010, Asin holds overall responsibility for the company's strategy, operations and growth on a global basis. He has been with the company since 2003, where he previously held the position of Chief Analyst, leading the team responsible for SIA's award-winning research and content. Asin is the co-author of *Breaking Through: Leadership Disciplines from Top Performing Staffing Firms* and is a frequent speaker at industry events, sharing essential insights on leadership and the challenges, opportunities and rapid transformations around work today. He is quoted in major business and industry publications, including the *New York Times, BusinessWeek, Inc. Magazine, The Atlantic, Bloomberg Business, CNBC, Marketplace, USA Today* and *MarketWatch* among others. Prior to joining SIA, Asin spent nearly 12 years as a senior executive at global staffing leader Adecco SA. Before Adecco, he held operations management positions with PepsiCo, and he began his professional career with Andersen Consulting, the predecessor of Accenture. He holds an M.B.A. from Harvard University and a B.S. in engineering from Princeton University.

Chance Welton (pages 69, 134, 136)

Chance Welton got his work ethic from his father. Raised on a potato farm in Idaho, he learned from an early age that whatever he was going to have in life was going to come from hard work. As Chance grew up, life taught him some hard lessons, and he became determined to provide for himself and those he loves– a life that he could previously only dream of. A self-made entrepreneur he is the owner and CEO of Beachwood Marketing, a 7-figure online marketing platform. He is also the co-founder of the "Modern Millionaires." The only complete digital business program that has taught hundreds of students how to build a digital business from scratch. He has been written up in publications like Forbes and Entrepreneur for his innovative mindset, determination, and ability to build everything out of nothing. Chance believes his success is rooted in the way he approaches life as well as business. By staying centered, putting the important pieces first, and always waking up before the sunrise.

Curtis Blodgett (pages 183, 184)

Curtis is an entrepreneur, opening up Beach Bee Meadery, a successful family business with his son Jackson in late 2019. He is an experienced global account manager with a demonstrated history of working in the information technology and services industry. Skilled in Software Sales, Storage Area Network (SAN), Enterprise Software, Storage, Customer Relationship Management (CRM), and Enterprise Account Management. Strong sales professional with a Bachelor of Arts (BA) focused in Computer Science from State University of New York College at Potsdam.

David Blake (page 125)

David has dedicated his life to the mission of changing the way the world learns and helping others evolve their thinking about learning and what it means to get an education. He co-founded Degreed, an education technology company, and has worked passionately and tirelessly to make this vision a reality. David is the Executive Chairman of Degreed and Managing Partner of Future of Work Studios. David is also CEO of Learn In, an upskilling-as-a-service platform helping companies with their large-scale internal upskilling initiatives.

David Callahan (pages 105, 106, 110)

David is the founder and editor of two digital media sites about public affairs: Inside Philanthropy and Blue Tent. He has written extensively on trends in philanthropy, as well as American politics and public policy. David is author, most recently, of *The Givers: Wealth, Power, and Philanthropy in a New Gilded Age*. Before launching Inside Philanthropy in 2014 and Blue Tent in 2020, David co-founded Demos, the national think tank, where he held various leadership positions and conducted research on a wide range of issues related to economic and political inequality, as well as writing on moral values, professional ethics and business. In addition to "The Givers," David is the author of seven widely-reviewed books on domestic and international issues, including *The Cheating Culture: Why More Americans Are Doing Wrong to Get Ahead*. He has appeared on hundreds of television and radio programs, including major networks and national NPR shows and published numerous op-ed and feature articles in such places as the New York Times and Washington Post. He has spoken at over 150 universities and associations around the U.S., frequently as a keynote speaker. David is a graduate of Hampshire College and received his Ph.D. from Princeton University, where he studied American politics and international relations. David lives in Santa Monica, California.

David Condra (pages 130, 131, 133, 134, 146)

David graduated from Vanderbilt University as an Electrical Engineer in 1969 and was sent to South Africa by his new employer, Southwire, to start up and run a cable manufacturing company. Returning to Southwire, with his new wife, Estelle from South Africa, David subsequently became vice president. In 1979 he founded Dalcon Computer Systems, subsequently named Amplion, an early pioneer in microcomputer systems and software for healthcare. In 2000 David was the first president of the Nashville Technology Council, and was founder of the Nashville Capital Network.

David Heinemeier Hansson (pages 195, 197, 198, 199, 202, 216)

David is the creator of Ruby on Rails[2], and co-founder & CTO at Basecamp, the saner, organized way to manage projects and communicate company-wide. He is the best-selling author of *It Doesn't Have to be Crazy at Work* and *ReWork*. David has raced in the FIA World Endurance Championship[3] for the past seven years. He is a frequent podcast guest and family man.

Day Veerlapati (page 220)

Dayakar "Day" Veerlapati is the President and CEO of S2Tech, an IT services company serving Medicaid programs in 35+ states. Launched in 1997, S2Tech has global headquarters in Chesterfield, Missouri, and regional development centers in Jefferson City, Missouri, and Hyderabad, India. S2Tech has a diversified clientele, growing profits, and high employee morale. Moreover, Day created the nonprofit Fortune Fund that has helped 100+ poor children in India earn college degrees and become software engineers, nurses, pharmacists and accountants. The Fund plans to expand to rural Missouri in 2021. Day earned Master's degrees in Industrial Engineering and Operations Research from the Indian Institute of Technology and in Information Management from Washington University in St. Louis.

---

2   https://dhh.dk/#rails
3   https://www.fiawec.com/

Diane Flynn (pages 63, 198)

Diane Flynn is Cofounder and CEO of ReBoot Accel, designing work cultures that support and promote women and underrepresented groups. She consults with Fortune 500 companies on diverse and inclusive cultures, and co-authored The Upside, presenting the business case for diverse workplaces and best practices for tapping the potential of women. She facilitates workshops on professional presence and impact, and coaches leaders on maximizing results and finding personal fulfillment. Diane previously served as Chief Marketing Officer of GSVlabs, a marketing executive at Electronic Arts, and an associate consultant at The Boston Consulting Group. She has spoken on Diversity, Ageism, and the Future of Work at venues including SXSW, Stanford GSB, and the Modern Elder Academy. She earned a BA in Economics from Stanford and an MBA from Harvard.

Dr. Jonathan Biggane (pages 95, 96, 97)

Dr. Biggane is an Associate Professor in the department of Management at California State University, Fresno. Prior to entering academia, Jonathan worked as a Senior Staffing Consultant at GE Nuclear, a Business Analyst at BHI Energy, and a Legislative Aide at the New York State Senate. He holds a PhD from the University of Memphis, MBA and BS in Management from the University of North Carolina Wilmington and he is completing a graduate degree at Harvard University's Extension School. Jonathan's research interests include intra-organizational relationships, with particular emphasis on employee well-being.

Dr. Madan Kataria (pages 175, 176)

Dr. Kataria is the founder and President at Laughter Yoga International. Dr. Kataria, a medical doctor from Mumbai, India popularly known as the 'Guru of Giggling' (London Times), is the founder of Laughter Yoga Clubs movement started in 1995. While researching the benefits of laughter, he was amazed by the number of studies showing the profound physiological and psychological benefits of laughter. He decided to find a way to deliver these benefits to his patients and other people. The result is Laughter Yoga, a unique exercise routine that combines group laughter exercises with yoga breathing which allows anyone to laugh without using jokes, humor or comedies. Started with just five people in a public park in Mumbai in 1995, it has grown into a worldwide movement of more than 16,000 Laughter Yoga clubs in over 110 countries. Spreading rapidly in USA, Canada, Europe, Australia, the Middle East, South East Asia, China and Africa, this new concept has been widely covered by prestigious publications like the TIME magazine, National Geographic, and the Wall Street Journal and featured on CNN, BBC, US networks and the Oprah Winfrey Show.

Dr. Shirley Davis (pages 131, 155)

Dr. Shirley Davis is an accomplished corporate executive and an award-winning global workforce expert, with over 30 years of business experience in a variety of senior leadership roles, including her last role of Vice President of Global Diversity and Inclusion for the Society for Human Resource Management. She's also a best-selling author, serves on several national boards, and is a popular facilitator for four LinkedIn Learning leadership courses.

Erica Kuhl (pages 257, 258, 259, 260, 271, 272)

Erica has over 18 years of enterprise community expertise. Formerly VP Community at Salesforce, she built everything from scratch from strategy and programs to metrics and ROI. She understands running community programs on any size budget and with any size team, large or small. She's also seen massive company growth from 176 to 49,000 employees allowing her to adapt strategies and deeply understand challenges at any stage.

Gary Bolles (page 78)

Global lecturer and writer on the future of work, learning, and the organization. Chair for the Future of Work with Singularity University; partner with Charrette.us, a San Francisco consulting firm catalyzing "initiatives with impact"; and co-founder of eParachute.com, from the insights of *What Color Is Your Parachute?*, the world's enduring career manual.

Gwendolyn Turner (pages 88, 213, 252)

Global Executive with experience driving diversity and social impact initiatives within various industries with revenues ranging from $10B–$50B. Proven experience creating, developing, and leading diversity and external relations functions in North America, United Kingdom, South Africa, and Asia. A corporate leader and business owner with a blended background of diversity strategy, entrepreneurship, and corporate citizenship experience. Helping companies innovate to become mom-friendly for working mothers through inclusive engagement strategies and talent development.

Ivica Jandrijević (pages 256, 266, 267)

Ivica is a graphic designer from Croatia who accidentally strayed into the world of books fifteen years ago and fell in love with the process of making them. Since then he has worked on more than 800 book titles in varying genres as a typographer, and as a book cover designer. He's designed covers for everyone from Stephen

R. Covey to Paula Hawkins. When he's not creating new fonts or taking award-winning landscape photos, Ivica takes his family hiking.

Jeff Gothelf (pages 79, 80)

Jeff helps organizations build better products and executives build the cultures that build better products. He is the co-author of the award-winning book *Lean UX* and the Harvard Business Review Press book, *Sense & Respond*. Starting off as a software designer, Jeff now works as a coach, consultant and keynote speaker helping companies bridge the gaps between business agility, digital transformation, product management and human-centered design. His most recent book, *Forever Employable*, was published in June 2020.

Jen Sargent (pages 141, 200, 220, 222, 223)

Jen Sargent has been an executive and entrepreneur in digital media for over 20 years. She was the CEO and co-founder of HitFix, a digital media brand focused on helping consumers discover, talk about and experience the movies, TV and pop culture they love. After HitFix was acquired by Uproxx Media Group, she was president for two years. Currently, Jen is the CEO of Wondery, a leading podcast publisher known for immersive audio storytelling with hits such as *The Apology Line, Business Wars, Even The Rich* and *Dr. Death*.

Jesse Draper (pages 47, 48)

Jesse Draper is a mother of two boys, founding partner of Halogen Ventures as well as creator and host of Emmy nominated television series, *The Valley Girl Show*. Draper is a fourth-generation venture capitalist focused on early stage investing in female founded consumer technology. She stars on SET's television series *Meet the*

Draper's currently in its fourth season. Draper was listed by *Marie Claire* magazine as one of the '50 Most Connected Women in America.' Draper has been a contributor to *Marie Claire*, *Mashable*, *Forbes*, and is a regular investor and tech personality on shows including TLC's *Girl Starter*, *The Katie Couric Show*, *Fox's Good Day LA*, CNBC's *Who Wants to Be the Next Millionaire Inventor?* and Freeform's *Startup U*. She proudly sits on the board of directors of Carbon38, Trust & Will, Preemadonna (creator of the Nailbot), and the non-profit board of Bizworld. Draper supports the Parkinson's Institute and is very involved with growing UCLA's female entrepreneurship community.

Jennifer McClure (page 173)

Jennifer McClure is an entrepreneur, keynote speaker, and high-performance coach who works with leaders to leverage their influence, increase their impact, and accelerate results. She's also the Chief Excitement Officer of DisruptHR, a global community designed to move the collective thinking forward when it comes to talent in the workplace, and hosts a weekly podcast called Impact Makers, featuring conversations with leaders who are changing the world in small and big ways.

Julie Sowash (page 62)

Julie Sowash, Executive Director of Disability Solutions, Co-Host of *Crazy and the King* podcast and international keynote speaker on greater inclusion for disability in our workplaces and in our world. As a founding member of Disability Solutions, Julie and her team build enterprise-wide strategy, brand, and solutions for local, national, and global companies committed to hiring talent with disabilities. Julie is also the Co-Host of the *Crazy and the King Podcast*, an honest and irreverent take on today's diversity, equity, inclusion and belonging topics. She is an advocate for intentional and thoughtful inclusion and belonging for all people with disabilities. Julie has spent nearly her entire adult life as a person with multiple mental illnesses. She is a graduate of Indiana University and lives in Columbus, Indiana with her wonderful husband, three children and dogs.

Julie Trell (pages 85, 86)

Julie Trell is the Country Lead, Australia, for SheEO. She's been challenging and inverting norms throughout her career, making waves with her fresh perspective and innovative thinking. When she redesigned a previous job title to 'Vice President of All Things Fun, Meaningful & Rewarding' at Salesforce Foundation, it was a powerful reinforcement of her values, which is integral to the workplace culture around her. Julie's career has centered around building connections between people, programs, and ecosystems.

Khurshed Batliwala (page 177)

Khurshed is a personal coach, author, TedX speaker, wellbeing expert, teacher of meditation for the Art of Living, and alternative healer. He has been invited to speak at corporate houses ranging from startups to Fortune 100 companies, and at universities in more than 35 countries. He has written two books (with Dinesh Ghodke) *Ready, Study, Go! – Smart Ways to Learn,* published by Harper Collins which has been translated into Hindi, Tamil and Bulgarian and *Happiness Express* published by Amazon-Westland. Together, both books have sold over 100,000 copies. As a personal coach, through his Deep Coaching program, he helps individuals to gain clarity and take strategic action towards their dreams and goals. He specializes in creating bespoke interventions that promote mental and emotional wellbeing for individuals and teams.

Kimberly Sneeder (pages 55, 56, 57, 210, 242)

Kim is an experienced and passionate leader with a demonstrated history of working in the recruiting industry serving underrepresented communities. Committed to digitally transforming the industry by providing an effective platform for education and upskilling opportunities. By partnering the best technical education companies with those individuals who want to position themselves for better opportunities, real progress can be made against the current skills gap.

Kip Wright (pages 132, 137)

Kip Wright is President & CEO of Genuent. Wright is a staffing industry veteran instrumental in shifting the landscape of the human capital industry. Known as a passionate leader with an innate ability to drive both growth and organizational efficiencies, Wright is responsible for all facets of executive strategy and leadership for Genuent. In his 26-year career, Wright has served in numerous leadership roles with public and private staffing and workforce solution companies, including Manpower, TAPFIN, COMSYS, and EY. Considered a leader in the field of human capital and workforce fulfillment, Wright is the recipient of numerous awards, and was recently inducted into Staffing Industry Analysts' "Staffing 100" award Hall of Fame, recognizing the most influential leaders in the staffing industry.

Lauren Deen (pages 107, 135)

Lauren Deen is a multiple Emmy and James Beard award winning television and digital executive producer and director, known for delivering high production value and high volume on budget; finding new talent both in front of and behind the camera; and working with unknown and celebrity talent through her company

Cake Productions, and other major corporations. Deen has developed, produced, and directed dozens of series for numerous networks including Martha Stewart, Food Network (developed and sold Next Food Network Star, created and directed the Emmy award-winning Grill It! With Bobby Flay), launched the Cooking Channel (Foodography with Mo Rocca, Emmy-nominated My Grandmother's Ravioli, Drink Up!), Lifetime's Cook Yourself Thin franchise, and helped launch the YouTube Hungry Channel. Deen is also a New York Times bestselling author of Cook Yourself Thin, and Cook Yourself Thin Faster, Kitchen Playdates, and The Meatball Shop. Information can be found on her website.[4]

Lisa Goldenthal (pages 169, 170)

Lisa G. is the best-selling author of *The Boss Weight Loss*, and creator of the original *Skinny Jeans Workout* that sold over 100,000 units in Target. Lisa has been featured in *Life & Style* Magazine, KTLA 5, CBS News, Thrive Global, and Web MD and has 20+ years transforming clients' lives, including Cheryl Tiegs and Paul Zane Pilzer. Lisa is recognized as an expert VIP lifestyle coach, creating customized nutrition and exercise plans for clients to combat sleep deprivation, stress and unhealthy eating. Lisa gets results for high-impact CEOs, Senior Executives, busy Entrepreneurs and Boss Moms by holding them to the highest level of accountability to get in shape while increasing productivity and energy levels. She inspires clients to go from stuck to unstoppable in all areas of life – wellness, weight loss, business and mindset. Lisa recently launched The WholeCEO Podcast where she sits down with industry leaders in business, wellness, fitness and mindset to discuss their insider secrets to being unstoppable, wrapped around their own personal journeys to dreaming bigger and never giving up…no matter what.

---

4   http://laurendeen.com/

Mara Swan (pages 243, 246, 247)

At ManpowerGroup, Mara had responsibility for global strategy, HR, marketing, risk management, PR, ESG, DEI, innovation and thought leadership. She also was responsible for their Right Management business segment. Mara has been a board member of GOJO Industries, a manufacturer of Purell and other hand hygiene products, since 2011. She joined BrightView Inc's board in 2019 and ULINE, North America's largest shipping and business supplies company board in 2020. Following her retirement in March 2020, she started Xceleration LLC, a human capital consulting business where she provides advice and services on human capital strategy, talent, DEI, compensation, workforce productivity and performance issues as well as CEO coaching.

In 2015, Mara was named as one of the 15 most influential and prominent women leading HR functions in the United States.

Michael Kreaden (pages 153, 156, 238)

Michael is a passionate startup advisor, with 20+ years of experience in enterprise SaaS. His background in technology evangelism is centered around platforms that have a profound impact on the way we create, manage and share information. His career has revolved around the Macintosh platform (1987-1995), the Internet and early ASPs (1995-2001) and the Salesforce Platform (2002-Present). Michael's personal mission is to accelerate success for startups targeting the Salesforce ecosystem.

Naeem Zafar (pages 79, 228)

Naeem Zafar has been teaching at the University of California, Berkeley since 2005. He is a Dean's Teaching Fellow, lecturer and Industry Fellow at the Center of Entrepreneurship and Technology.

He is also an adjunct professor at Northeastern University. He teaches courses in Entrepreneurship, Technology Strategy, Innovation and New Venture Finance. Naeem is also a serial entrepreneur and currently the co-founder and CEO of TeleSense, a company creating solutions in the AgTech space. Naeem has authored five books on entrepreneurship. Information can be found on his website.[5]

Scott Jorgensen (pages 182, 186)

Scott leads a world-class team of ecosystem, content, and program experts who ensure that all AppExchange ISV partners and ISV Sales teams have the knowledge and skills required to play their roles in growing the Salesforce ecosystem. He develops Salesforce's enablement system to identify and measure enablement needs, produce relevant content and curriculum, and distribute both through programs that reach an audience of internal teams, partner technical and business leaders, architects, marketers and sales teams. As a builder and innovator, Scott has influenced strategic innovation at Salesforce. In 2009, he developed Salesforce's CIO Advisory Board program and served as the meeting chair through 2018. Scott is also a founding member of the Salesforce Ignite Program, a customer innovation program that introduced design thinking to Salesforce customers to create and grow customer-centric business models. He led Ignite for seven years before standing-up the Salesforce Office of Innovation in 2018 by teaming Ignite with the Salesforce Futures Lab and partnering with YPO (Young President's Organization). As a passionate champion of equality and diversity, Scott serves as an advisory board member of Mom Relaunch, a startup, whose mission is to bridge the gap between mothers returning to their careers and the need for skilled talent and diversity in the workforce.

---

5   www.NaeemZafar.com

Scott Gordon (pages 62, 63, 248)

As Vice President of Talent Solutions, Scott prides himself on lending his deep Vacotian knowledge to more than 400+ recruiters in all specialties across the globe. He works one-on-one with our local managing partners to implement the most innovative and effective recruiting approach to each specific market. As a leader of leaders, Scott enables managing partners and recruiters to continuously improve and grow as advocates for candidates and as contributing members of the Vaco family. He prides himself on his "24/7, always-on, mountain-moving" brand of service, and believes that making a successful placement is so much more than finding someone a job. The right placement can be life-changing, and that's a business Scott's happy to be in.

Stephan Spencer (pages 159, 161, 162, 163, 165)

Stephan Spencer is an SEO expert, serial entrepreneur, Internet luminary and life hacker. He's the founder of interactive agencies Netconcepts and Stephan Spencer and has created a unique pay-for-performance SEO technology. Stephan is author of the acclaimed *The Art of SEO, Social eCommerce, and Google Power Search*. He's optimized the websites of some of the biggest brands in the world, including Chanel, Volvo, Sony, and Zappos. Stephan hosts two popular podcast shows: *Get Yourself Optimized* and *Marketing Speak*, which Apple selected as one of iTunes' "new & noteworthy" podcasts.

Stu Heinecke (pages 144, 145, 146, 147, 148, 213, 236)

Author/Host/Marketer/WSJ cartoonist Stu was named the "Father of Contact Marketing" by the American Marketing Association, my mission is to provide unfair advantages to help enterprise/SMB/

startup sales teams get more C-level meetings with top accounts faster and more effectively using contact marketing principles revealed in my two bestselling books, How to Get a Meeting with Anyone (2016) and Get the Meeting! (2019). Agency/Strategy/Campaign Review/Consulting. Stu is the host of the How to Get a Meeting with Anyone podcast. In this podcast, Heinecke asks a simple question to each of his guests: "When you absolutely must break through to someone of great importance, someone who's nearly impossible to reach, how do you do it?"

Ted Capshaw (pages 104, 106, 119, 210)

Prior to starting his own company focused on leadership and culture development 11 years ago, Ted served as a Chief Learning Officer at several companies. He also was the Chief Operating Officer of a well known Non Profit Organization in Baltimore. Ted spends the majority of his time coaching individuals and teams in such areas as leadership, communication, personal development, building trust, operating more effectively and efficiently and daring people to live a more integrated, fulfilling, and prosperous life. He is known for his very real and hard hitting insights that he delivers with an unwavering intent to help and promote change. And, simply put in his words… "He cares…a lot." Ted studied sociology at the University of Minnesota and Human Development in Graduate School at St. Mary's University of Minnesota. He also notes that one of the more impactful learning experiences he has had was being accepted into and completing the Greater Baltimore Committee's Leadership program in 2011. Ted and his wife, Angel, have two sons, Jaxon and Maxwell, and live in Westminster, MD.

Tim Draper (pages 201, 232)

Timothy Cook Draper, is an American venture capital investor, and founder of Draper Fisher Jurvetson (DFJ),[6] Draper University, Draper Venture Network, Draper Associates[7] and Draper Goren Holm. His most prominent investments include Baidu, Hotmail, Skype, Tesla, SpaceX, AngelList, SolarCity, Ring, Twitter, DocuSign, Coinbase, Robinhood, Ancestry.com, Twitch, Cruise Automation, and Focus Media. Tim has authored *When A Venture Capitalist Enters California's Political Matrix: Innovation Meets The Status Quo*, 2018 and *How to be The Startup Hero: A Guide and Textbook for Entrepreneurs and Aspiring Entrepreneurs*, 2017. Awards: WEF's "Entrepreneur for the World, Commonwealth Club's "Distinguished Citizen," Independent Institute's "Toqueville Liberty Award," Forbes' "Midas List. Worth's "100 Most Powerful People in Finance." Top 100 most influential Harvard Alumni. AlwaysON's #1 Networked Venture Capitalist.

Vinita Gupta (page 185)

In her early career, Vinita worked as an engineer for GTE Lenkurt and later held engineering management positions at Bell Northern Research (now part of Nortel Networks). In May 1985 she founded Digital Link Corporation, a company which engaged in the design, manufacture, marketing, and support of digital wide-area network access products for global networks. The company went public in 1994 and was later renamed as Quick Eagle Networks. Vinita still serves as chairman, chief executive officer and president. Vinita serves as chairman of Palo Alto Medical Foundation Research Institute. She also serves on the board of Indian School of Business (ISB), Hyderabad and Cancer Prevention Institute of California.

---

6   https://en.wikipedia.org/wiki/Tim_Draper#cite_note-HBSbio-3
7   https://en.wikipedia.org/wiki/Tim_Draper#cite_note-4

She is credited with being the first woman of Indian origin to take her company public in the United States.

Wendy Paris (pages 72, 142)

Wendy Paris is the author of *Splitopia: Dispatches from Today's Good Divorce* and *How to Part Well* (Simon & Schuster, 2016), and the co-author of *Buy the Change You Want to See: Use Your Purchasing Power to Make the World a Better Place* (Penguin Random House, 2019). She was also the writer on the book *Big Kibble: The Hidden Dangers of the Pet Food Industry* and How to Do Better by Our Dogs (St. Martin's Press, 2020). She has written for many publications, including *The New York Times, Psychology Today* and *The National Book Review*. She also works as a ghostwriter and book coach.

PART ONE

REALIZE
WHO ARE YOU AND HOW YOU GOT HERE

Being at a career crossroads can be scary, but this is also a rare opportunity to open yourself up to new possibilities.

In the first section, Realize, you will take the external circumstances that led you here into account, but most importantly, do a deep dive to connect with who you are and what kind of work makes you feel alive.

In the past you may have felt like a passive player in your career trajectory, but if you commit to doing the personal development work in this section, you will put yourself in the driver's seat. The work requires humility and taking ownership of your situation. If you bring a willingness to confront your weak spots and accept responsibility for the past, you'll begin to pave an intentional path toward achieving your goals and excelling in whatever it is you choose to do.

ONE DOOR CLOSES

"One of the hardest things in life to learn is which bridges to cross and which bridges to burn."

~ Oprah Winfrey

GROWING UP, I was lucky to get valuable advice from my parents, advice I internalized over the years. Out of several wise nuggets from my dad, I clearly remember hearing this one very often, "When one door closes, another one opens." Of course, as a child, I never understood the deep meaning of this concept. Thinking back, it was such a powerful way to encourage us to try new things and not give up if one path does not work out.

Oftentimes, the work we do becomes part of our identity, which is why getting fired or laid off can feel so upsetting. Because we are human, we often take it quite personally. We experience getting let go as a rejection of our ideas, our performance, and our abilities.

If this has happened to you, you are in good company. JK Rowling, Oprah Winfrey, and Walt Disney have all been fired. Even Steve Jobs was fired from Apple, the company he founded, in 1985. I include myself in this club as well because in early 2002 when I was working as Chief Technical Architect for a tech startup in Nashville, my boss, ex-mayor Phil Bredesen sold the company to McGraw Hill. I was let go just after my maternity leave, which felt terrible. I still remember the conversation with Phil. He told me that sometimes a turn of events can feel disappointing, though ultimately, it may turn into a hidden opportunity.

In the back of my mind, I remembered my dad's words, so I did not let that moment define me. In hindsight, I can see that if I had stayed at that job for ten years, I might have never started my own company. Now that I had a baby, I wanted more work flexibility and I found that I was able to pivot. Within two months I founded Avankia. To this day I am grateful to Phil for hiring me when he did, and for letting me go when he did.

Alexander Graham Bell spoke about failure, not as a negative, but as part of a process of trying new things. He noted that after a door closes, "We often look so long and so regretfully upon the closed door that we do not see the one which has opened for us." In my experience, this is one of the most common causes of depression. If you focus on something you tried that did not work out and you label yourself a failure it can become a self-fulfilling prophecy.

If indeed, a door has been closed in your professional life, it's important to examine why. The discussion and exercises in this chapter will help you process your situation, and most importantly will encourage you to find new opportunities and open the next door.

Let's take a look at different door-closing scenarios:

Laid off / Furloughed

There are times when a company's needs change, or an employee just isn't a fit, and for whatever reason, you get laid off. There have been devastating mortgage crises, terrorist attacks like the one we commemorate every 9/11, and a global pandemic that began in 2020. All of these had a massive impact on the economy. When you look at a thirty-year graph of unemployment in the United States from 1990 to 2020[8], it looks like a roller coaster ride, and it can feel like one if you're part of those statistics. It is hard to emphasize how much the ripple effects of these downturns in the economy are felt months, and even years later.

What happened in your case? Most employers give detailed information during layoffs. If the company is downsizing, then all the more reason to probe why you were selected, and not your colleagues. Layoffs can happen because of downsizing, recession, a department getting shut down, mergers, outsourcing, etc. Whatever the reason, figure out what role you may have played. Why were you chosen to be laid off over someone else? There may be mistakes you can learn from here.

If you were furloughed, assume that you are not being asked back. Use that time proactively. Work on your *hireability*. Learning is a constant process, whether it's earning degrees, reading articles, or attending webinars or workshops. Always keep your eyes open for job opportunities you might pursue if you are not called back to your job. Be sure to read the Lifelong Learning chapter, which

---

[8] https://www.bls.gov/web/empsit/cps_charts.pdf

goes into great depth about how you can curate your skills and education and continually learn and grow.

Getting laid off can trigger feelings of rejection and can spur insecurity. Acknowledge how you are feeling, but don't dwell on these emotions. If you played a part in getting laid off, you must learn what you did and do things differently in your next job. It's quite possible that this was a tough decision for the company, having little or nothing to do with your performance.

Getting Fired

This happens primarily because of lack of performance, productivity, not being a team player, creating a toxic work environment, or violating company policy. Or you may have simply touched a nerve and pissed off the wrong person. Whatever the reason is, getting fired is usually a direct reflection of your work style and professionalism. Of course, getting fired can trigger feelings of rejection and even shame, but again, acknowledge how you feel and then take a look in the mirror and deal with the reality in front of you. Own any role you may have played in this turn of events.

Being in the management role, I know how difficult it is to tell someone that he or she is fired. However, it is disappointing when the one who is let go is so quick to point to external factors—colleagues, company management, etc.—rather than owning any kind of responsibility for the situation. Are there obstacles and challenges within yourself that you need to work on? If you are unwilling to do the hard work and reflect on how your performance could have been improved, you are not only missing a very important lesson, but you are likely to repeat the same behavior at your next position and you may wind up in the very same unhappy situation of being let go a few years down the road.

Business *Not* as Usual

If you are a business owner, especially a small, bootstrapped business, then you are always concerned about the impact of external factors. You may have to close your business through no fault of your own. According to a McKinsey report, "30 million small-business jobs are vulnerable, and firms with fewer than a hundred employees are the hardest hit."[9] This situation is incredibly challenging to deal with since small business owners are so emotionally and financially immersed in their business that it makes it very difficult to manage. Once again, look for the reason it happened, the why, and learn from the experience.

Have the Tough Conversations

Reach out to trustworthy former colleagues and take them to lunch. Ask for some honest feedback regarding your work style, work performance, and things you might have done differently. Try to listen without letting your ego get in the way. Don't be defensive or deflect blame. Simply hear them out. It's never easy to listen to things you don't want to hear, but it is critical that you are able to accept constructive criticism. It will serve you well and open your eyes to areas that need improvement.

* * * *

One of the most important aspects of a door closing is the reflection that you do afterward. There is nothing that can be done to change the past, but reflecting on a situation, your role in it, and

---

[9] https://www.mckinsey.com/industries/public-and-social-sector/our-insights/covid-19s-effect-on-jobs-at-small-businesses-in-the-united-states

what you hope to achieve now that this door is closed is critical. Look to the future and start to plan your next move.

> **Assessing and Reflecting after a Door Is Closed**

1. List the reasons why your door closed. Interview colleagues for their opinion of your performance.
2. Is there a pattern that you can identify in your employment history? If yes, how do you think you can break this pattern? If this is your first time, can you think of anything you could have done differently to avoid being in this situation?
3. Where do you see yourself in two years; five years; ten years? How can you start to strategize a plan to get there? Start with small steps.

CONSCIOUSLY UNCOUPLING FROM YOUR CAREER

"Close some doors today. Not because of pride, incapacity, or arrogance, but simply because they lead you nowhere."

~ Paulo Coelho

IN THE LAST chapter, we talked about the external factors that lead to career crossroads. Now, let's talk about where you are in your life, and why you and your career may be "breaking up." If you are working in a career for ten, fifteen, or more years there is a good chance that either you have changed, your priorities have changed, you have outgrown your job, or all of the above. And then, there is career burnout, which can take a real toll on your mental and physical health.

In my experience, I have been extremely fortunate to work in a career that I am passionate about. I have done work that has fulfilled me and enriched my life, and I always recommend this path to the candidates I coach. Yes, financial stability is important, of course, and not everyone is an entrepreneur. Regardless, if you recognize that your life is out of balance, I firmly believe that you can control your own destiny by proactively seeking out a happier, healthier situation. Just by doing that you've already raised your morale a few notches.

A Modern Problem

Career burnout is an emerging concept. It is a result of opportunity. When I say that, I am considering my ancestors, and yours, and how the concept of work has morphed over the years from a situation that was supposed to bring in income to a situation that is also supposed to bring fulfillment. If you are a baby boomer or gen-X-er, you are probably the first generation to experience career burnout. When our parents and grandparents were starting out there were far fewer opportunities than we have now. Opportunities for people of color or for women were limited. There was less attention paid to things like diversity and pay equity. There was no internet. Let's take a three-dimensional look at the problem of career burnout.

Many professions are demanding. Some professions are demanding for the entire duration. Even when you work your way up, the level of intensity never really eases up. Not even when you gain a higher position. Perhaps, due to budget cuts, staff was reduced, and your workload got more and more difficult to manage. Unfortunately, some work environments are unfriendly and unpleasant. Perhaps your ideas are not given the respect they deserve, and you are treated unfairly. In some organizations there is a top-down toxicity and morale is low and the work culture simply does not feel inclusive or positive.

You've Outgrown Your Job

Sometimes a job that was once fulfilling and challenging plateaus, or changes. People are not cars—if you are coasting, or on autopilot at work, it's quite possible you have outgrown your job. In a *Fast Company* article Gwen Moran writes, "When you're coasting, you may get to the end of your day and realize that you went through the motions without a lot of focus or thought. It's the workplace equivalent of driving home and not remembering what route you took."[10] She goes on to quote executive coach Michael O'Brien, who explained that when you are not really being stretched, you probably have captured what the job has to offer in terms of knowledge, competencies, and skills.

Malaise

It's quite possible you may be experiencing dissatisfaction in your life. But rather than pin most of it on your job, perhaps you should

---

[10] https://www.fastcompany.com/90373222/4-telltale-signs-youve-outgrown-your-job-and-what-to-do-about-it

examine other areas of your life—family, friends, romantic relationships. Where are you not feeling fulfilled? If you are restless, the first step you need to take is to identify where that restlessness comes from.

You may be stuck in comparison mode, comparing yourself either to peers or to others in your profession and measuring yourself against them. It is important to remember that you cannot look for external validation, because it will never be satisfying in the long run. A feeling of success comes when you are aligned with your own values and goals. You must honor your journey and not always race to quantifiable results that you can brag about on your social media.

Is It the Job, or the Career?

If you've established that it's time to move on, it's important to distinguish between dissatisfaction with your organization and dissatisfaction with the nature of your industry. If you're going to make a lateral move to a company with a similar work culture and a similar level of intensity to the one that is currently stressing you out, you should not just be looking at switching jobs, you should be looking at switching careers.

Unrequited Loyalty

A long career is a marriage of sorts. Sometimes when you stay with an organization for a long time you feel a sense of loyalty. Unfortunately, that loyalty may turn out to be a one-way street. And though it is quite possible that the company you work for, your colleagues, and your boss, have positively impacted your career, that does not mean you should ignore telltale signs that you've grown all you can, and that the job no longer fits you. Staying in any situation out of allegiance usually means you are not being true to your own wants and needs because you are honoring the wants and needs of others above your own. If you've done the introspection and examined all angles and you know your situation is not good for you, you owe it to yourself to move on.

Instead of worrying about what will happen if you leave, worry instead about the health impact and the work-life imbalance that will surely happen if you stay.

If You Cannot Take a Break, Take a Breath

If you don't have a clear path to leaving your current job, accept that it is not the right moment to make a move. This is an excellent time for capital-L Learning. Pursue a degree online at night, or sharpen a talent that you have not utilized, or poke around in an area you want to pursue but previously had no time for. These days there are so many new ways to learn, outside of traditional degrees. There are so many ways to remain relevant in your field. There are books to read, eBooks, and whitepapers. You can participate in workshops, seminars, and masterminds. Take online courses. You may choose to work with a coach and take baby steps toward your goal before you take that leap. If you raise your own awareness, you are consciously making an effort to know what is behind that door, meaning you are helping create your own opportunities. This is a great feeling because you are not a pawn in someone else's game—you are empowering yourself to get into a better situation.

I spoke to Jesse Draper, founding partner of Halogen Ventures, who was able to identify that her lifestyle and priorities changed after getting married and having a baby. She chose that juncture to switch away from doing something she was burning out on. I asked how Jesse was able to achieve clarity on her next move while she was pregnant with her first child.

I loved doing what I was doing, but with the tech talk show, The Valley Girl *that I had started up, I was working around the clock, and we had struggles in so many areas, including getting the network to pay us. Also, on the side, I was making some investments in women-owned ventures, and that started kind of taking off. I had created this great network of women in tech, and so I pitched five hundred potential investors, closed fifty, and raised our first fund. So, I never stopped. I just kind of kept going. I grew up in a family of entrepreneurs. I don't know how to stop, but I know how to pivot.*

I was so impressed that Jesse was able to recognize she was burning out, but she took the passion and the connections from the tech talk show and launched women-owned businesses. This has not only been extremely successful, it has also furthered the cause she was so passionate about.

Growing up, I didn't see any women in technology or female CEOs around me. In order to change that, I created Halogen Ventures.

Jesse's story is a great example of how you can consciously uncouple from a career and pivot to one that is not only financially rewarding, but also resonates with your values as well.

* * * *

Big life decisions are often fraught with anxiety, and rightly so. Take time to assess the root cause of your desire to move on from your job. Explore all the internal and external factors that led up to this feeling, start mapping out a strategy and move on.

Assess the Internal and External Reasons for Wanting to Move on from Your Job

1. Do some introspection to try to evaluate the cause of your dissatisfaction at work. If you have identified external forces that are making you unhappy, brainstorm some possible solutions.

2. Is there a scenario where you stay at your job and make some changes? If this is worth exploring, perhaps you can arrange a meeting at work to discuss the possibilities.

3. If you are resolved to break up with your job, envision a new career. Do you feel good about it? Does it feel satisfying? Does it feel more aligned with your values and your skills? Can you see yourself growing there?

PARENTAL INDECISION

*"Whether or not to have a kid is perhaps
the biggest and toughest choice of your life,
because it's the only irreversible choice."*

~ Stephanie Reyes

THE BIGGEST, AND usually happiest, disruptor of your career is having a baby. But increasingly, there is trepidation and indecision about becoming a parent for people in their thirties and forties. We live in a pro-natalist society. Women are taught from early on that they will someday be mothers. Until more recent times, choice in this matter was never implied, and though it has improved a bit, there is still a stigma attached to people who end up choosing a child-free life.

And while having a family was always considered an extra expense, that cost—not to mention the limitations of many people's health insurance—has skyrocketed. When you consider that, on average, a family may expect to spend $233,610 ($284,570 if projected inflation costs are factored in*) for food, shelter, and other necessities to raise a child through age seventeen,[11] and the average cost of tuition, fees, and housing at a four-year private college is $200,000,[12] the financial burden is extremely sobering.

After marrying and moving to the states, it was four years before my husband, Rajeev, and I decided to have a child, which was cutting it close and raising some serious eyebrows back home in our traditional families! We always knew we wanted to raise a family together, but we were also very practical in how we went about it. We decided in advance that when we had a certain dollar-amount cushion in the bank we would be ready to take that plunge, and that is exactly what we did.

For this chapter, I was excited to sit down and speak with Ann Davidman, California Licensed Marriage and Family Therapist, motherhood clarity mentor, and author who wrote a very insightful book with Denise L. Carlini called, *Motherhood – Is It for Me? Your Step-by-Step Guide to Clarity.*

Mardy S. Ireland writes in the foreword of the book, "Regardless if you make motherhood happen—or you don't—the arc of your life will be significantly etched by this decision. This decision

---

[11] https://www.usda.gov/media/blog/2017/01/13/cost-raising-child
[12] https://www.fool.com/student-loans/heres-average-cost-private-college-today/

is such a "big deal" that some women simply deny it and pretend it's not something they have to deal with and external circumstances will decide for them."[13]

Similar to the modern phenomenon of career burnout, parental indecision is a concept that started to be discussed more openly among Gen X. When I spoke with Ann, she noted that increasingly, in the last ten years, in addition to the typical thirty and forty-somethings, she is seeing younger people in their late twenties reach out to her for help. And though this is an issue that couples may have to deal with together, Ann works with the individual. Both partners need to do the work separately, to know their own desire before they can work the situation out together.

In her practice, Ann has found that when you are dealing with what your heart wants combined with the pressures of the current realities of your life, anxiety starts to snowball to the point of total gridlock.

The work is not about listing pros and cons. It's so important to separate out all the noise and get in touch with your heart's desire.

That takes three to four months, according to Ann.

When you do that work, you are not in reaction to external forces, you're operating from authentic self-realization, and the importance of this cannot be stressed enough.

When you really sort out the "why," that drives your desire, you get grounded in a place that allows you to have clarity. When you make a decision, it may be that you want to be a parent, but not for four more years. And in that case, you can always go back to your why and understand where you are operating from. You may decide that you would like to become a parent, but only if certain conditions are met.

---

[13] Carlini, Denise L., Ann Davidman, and Mardy S. Ireland. *Motherhood: Is It For Me? Your Step-by-Step Guide to Clarity*. York, PA: Transformation Books, 2016.

Or, it may become clear when you do the work that you choose not to become a parent.

When Ann sees clients who are truly tortured by indecision, she advises them that if they cannot move forward, they must take a step back in order to move forward.

Once the clients who Ann works with are able to achieve some clarity, she coaches them on how to maintain that internal spaciousness. This is a term I learned from her that really resonated with me. Once you are in touch with your desire, you can revisit the parenthood decision later in life. With that sense of calm, you'll then be able to move forward and come to whatever decision is right for you.

Women and men both experience pressure around this subject, though it can manifest on different fronts. For men, there may be pressure from family to carry on the family name. Men and women feel societal pressure to take the conventional route, and hit all the milestones: start your career, meet Mr. or Mrs. Right, get married, have children. It can be very difficult for single people or young married people to imagine changing everything about their lives to accommodate having a child. The financial ramifications as well as the drastic change in lifestyle can definitely be daunting.

Not only do women experience societal and family pressure to have a baby, but they are also dealing with undeniable biological pressure as well. The biological clock that ticks away for women in their thirties and then begins to sound alarm bells at forty ticks alongside the career clock for women, who often feel torn to choose one path over the other. For this reason, forty-three percent of women take a career break—many of them in the prime of their career. Of those women, seventy percent eventually return to work—but only forty percent come back full time.[14]

---

[14] https://www.nbcnews.com/know-your-value/feature/rise-stay-home-working-mom-ncna987371

For the perspective of the person on a career track grappling with parental indecision, I interviewed two women who completely related, Kim Sneeder, who has been down that road, and Ashley Connell, who is in the throes of her own parental indecision.

Kim was on a successful career trajectory with one company for twenty-two years. She started out as a recruiter, then she worked in local sales, moving up to work in national sales. Kim told me about her climb up the career ladder.

It's probably a pretty rare scenario, but my first job out of college wound up being a place I stayed with for two decades. When I moved into a national sales position, I was traveling fifty out of fifty-two weeks in a year. So, in my late thirties, though I absolutely loved what I was doing, it was not conducive to settling down and starting a family. I really did struggle with parental indecision. I sort of kept thinking, "next year." And then next year became, "next year." I really didn't see it as putting off having a family, I saw it as prioritizing my career. Then suddenly at forty, I woke up and knew I had to focus all my attention on having a baby. Rich and I were determined to have a family, and we made it happen, though it was not easy. I was struggling to balance a demanding career with starting a family, and of course, after we had children there were new challenges trying to manage it all.

Kim, like many people pursuing a career in her twenties and thirties, had different priorities at different stages of her life. And though she always enjoyed a very successful and challenging profession, Kim was able to make career shifts that accommodated her personal priorities. When her mother fell ill, she made a shift from sales to operations that allowed her to spend all of her time at her home base instead of traveling.

Her story is so inspiring because rather than giving up a challenging career that she loved, she was able to reinvent herself over the twenty-two years she spent working for the same company. In my experience, it is very rare to see someone who is able to remain in one organization that long. But it was the perfect situation for Kim because there was such a deep legacy of built-in support for her to accommodate different needs at each stage of her career. Ironically, her current position would not have been offered to her had she not taken that role in operations.

Every time I made a big change it did feel risky, and scary, but with a new set of experiences, I'm happy to say I was able to drive change in a massive way. It's almost like I had to get out of my own way to get there.

Ashley Connell's parental indecision is similar in that she, too, is never sure when that magical "right time" will be to step back from Prowess, the company she founded, to get pregnant, have a baby, and raise a child. She was very open about acknowledging what an extreme lifestyle change this would be for her and her husband Matt, and also what a considerable financial undertaking it would be. Like Rajeev and I back in the early 2000s, Matt and Ashley have a number they need to get to in order to break into that financial comfort zone where they can be sure they have enough money saved for their kids' education and all the other living costs. And, like Kim, Ashley knows that her career trajectory coincides with that biological clock, something constantly hanging over her head.

Are we financially ready? Does one of us at least have great health insurance? Am I professionally where I need to be? We got married after having been together ten years, and that was a big part of moving to the next step but getting married wasn't nearly the same pressure as the fact that I have a ticking time bomb which is my ovaries—he does not! I understand how this isn't as pressing for him but being open about being really scared about that was key. In my parental indecision, I am leaning more and more toward wanting to make it work and being committed to making this work because I always had a sense that we could be great parents together. We balance each other out really well.

Guilt is also an emotion that comes up for women grappling with parental indecision. Women often put a lot of pressure on themselves. There's the guilt of being a working mom, the guilt of not being a mom, as well as guilt you're stepping off the career ladder and somehow blowing your opportunities.

After hearing Ashley and Kim's stories, I thought back to grappling with this decision when I was in my twenties. For my husband and me, there was careful deliberation, but there were so many factors to take into consideration. I was at the prime of my early career, working as Chief Technical Architect at a startup, an accomplishment I was very proud of. We both knew for certain that we wanted to have kids, but the big question was when. Being immigrants in this country, we knew that whatever step we took, we would have to be ready for this responsibility on all fronts. We knew that sadly, we did not have the family support we would have had back in India.

Of course, we are all familiar with the notion that it takes a village to raise a family, but unfortunately, the communal way of living has become a thing of the past. It's so important for anyone thinking of starting a family, whether they are new to this country or born and raised here, to try to recreate that village. There are so many other new parents that need support. If you can help each other even just to coordinate some playdates while one person takes a meeting or has a chance to go to a movie with her spouse, that can be a big thing.

* * * *

There isn't another decision you make in your life that will be as impactful as deciding to become a parent. It usually brings a lot of joy but struggling with the decision can feel like a weight. If you are grappling with parental indecision, do some introspection. Imagine what your life would be like after a child comes into your world. How will this impact your career, your relationship, your finances? Are you ready to take the plunge?

Assessing Parental Indecision

1. Are you in parental indecision mode? If yes, what factors are influencing you? List internal and external elements. If you have a partner, is he/she on the same page?

2. Would you take a career break? Is your career flexible? Are there things you would do differently work-wise to accommodate having children?

3. If you have decided to have a child, let's work on a high-level action plan for your career. How will you absorb this change into your home and work life?

GETTING BACK IN THE GAME

"It's a great moment in history because technology has created an infinite horizon for work possibilities. Opportunities are all around us, we just need to grab them, shape them, and forge a path forward."

~ Reena Gupta

THE WORLD OF work is morphing, and technology is indeed moving at a rapid pace. All of this can feel quite intimidating for someone reentering the workforce after a career break. While it's true that the industry you once knew has shifted, it's important to focus on all the soft skills you honed during the years you stepped away. Technical skills can always be sharpened, and there are plenty of courses you can take to bridge your skills gap; those are rarely a big deal. But the life skills you acquired and mastered, irrespective of what you did while on a career break are also incredibly valuable. Never sell yourself short on all that you were able to accomplish when you stepped away from work.

In my work at Mom Relaunch, one thing that stands out when I talk to the candidates is how many of them have lost confidence in themselves. If you took time off to raise children, you should be proud that you have now worked (and succeeded) at the hardest job on Earth! You have juggled several people's schedules, accommodated the needs of many people simultaneously, and you walked the fraught emotional terrain of nurturing, guiding, and disciplining that are part of the daily challenges of raising capable and independent children. This is no small thing, and though it is rare for parenting skills to be acknowledged, in my personal experience, they are absolutely useful and transferable skills.

If during this time you worked as a volunteer running book fairs, at scout programs, school auctions, or literacy programs, you learned concrete, transferable skills—team management, fundraising, or liaising with different organizations, etc. These things build to form a cumulative whole that is much stronger than you realize.

The process I've developed in our Mom Relaunch program addresses this emotional issue and boosts confidence by augmenting skills with hands-on experience. The nurturing and mentoring aspect of the program is essential to ease people back into the workforce. I also stress to my candidates the importance of having an open mind about their job prospects and capabilities.

On the corporate/company side, the work I do involves educating our partners on the value of candidates who are not as visibly represented—people with resume gaps and people from diverse backgrounds. I am not in the business of asking for charity from these companies. I provide value. When they become an ally, they will be hiring talented, trained people who are ready to give their best.

Our four-step process includes:

1. Career Assessment — Meet with an advisor. Based on your background and expectations, your advisor will help you to craft a personalized career plan.

2. Training & Certification — Depending on several factors (work experience, time away from work, etc.), you will be assigned a training plan through our proprietary Mom Relaunch Learning Management System. Your training consists of online/virtual instruction from different partners in our program. If we determine that you do not need any training, you may be directly assigned to a project to gain hands-on experience. You will also be assigned to a peer mentor who will guide you on your journey.

3. Launchpad — You will gain hands-on work experience and boost your confidence. You will work on several real-world projects, apply the job skills you learned, and most importantly boost your confidence by working on projects in a simulated company environment.

4. Placements & Projects — After you complete your Launchpad program, Mom Relaunch will help place you in a suitable job or project. Many of our candidates prefer flexible or remote work. We get projects and job placement leads from partnerships with leading organizations and companies. We will prepare and mentor you. We want you to put your best foot forward.

In the past, getting companies to allow my candidates to work remotely was a challenge, but the global pandemic of 2020 has altered this landscape.

Julie Sowash of Disability Solutions has done an amazing job integrating talent from different backgrounds into the workforce. Julie agreed with my point about the pandemic. Ironically, she feels it has been a positive disruptor.

What we've seen over the past six months is that suddenly the whole world became disabled—we couldn't physically get to work, we couldn't take the kids in, you have to wear masks everywhere—and, interestingly enough, companies that told us for decades, "We are <u>not</u> a work from home culture," are overnight reinventing at light speed and bending all the rules to adapt to the new normal because the world demanded it. Suddenly companies are coming to the realization that the world we've built so far is not inclusive of everyone's needs and abilities. The pandemic has given us a chance to create a better, more inclusive, work culture.

I also spoke with Scott Gordon, Vice President of Talent Solutions at Vaco, for his take on returning to the workforce. Scott emphasized that as an employee:

No matter who you are, how old you are, or whether you're coming back from a career break—the bottom line is, what the clients I work with care about is making money, saving money, and saving time. Companies need people who can produce.

Both Scott and Julie reiterated the importance of returning candidates having an open mind. If you have tunnel vision, you're not using your peripheral vision to open yourself up to different possibilities. Julie had a great insight into the concept of reinvention.

If you're not intellectually curious—curious about process and technology—you're going to get stuck. You've got to be nimble—open to learning new things. When people think about reinvention it is such a huge thing, but in reality, for most of us, reinvention is incremental. One skill opens up curiosity about another skill, and that can steer you on a different course. It's not necessarily 1,000% epic and transformational, it's something you build steadily on every day.

In today's world, knowledge is not confined solely to the ambit of those with the resources to afford it. Education has been democratized. There is definitely a tendency for people who stepped off the career track to focus on how they have been left behind, or on how they may now be out of touch. The good news is, there are so many different ways to bridge skill gaps and remain relevant these days, and many of these don't involve spending hundreds of thousands of dollars. Anyone can learn if he or she is interested and committed.

Diane Flynn, co-founder, and CEO of ReBoot Accel echoed my sentiments about the benefits employers receive when they hire a woman transitioning back into the workforce.

When companies hire our candidates, they're often surprised by the huge upside—pattern recognition. By virtue of being older and experienced (even if not paid for gaining this experience), they are able to anticipate things, they're often calm under pressure, and they bring great wisdom to the role. They tend to be very well connected and loyal. Many are seeking meaningful engagement and willing to find the right fit. We often see that millennials spend eighteen months on average at a job, while these women are often in it for the long haul.

When you apply for jobs, you should approach the job search with intention, plan, and strategize. When I asked Scott about the interviewing process, he had this to say:

Don't randomly sling resumes out there. Be thoughtful. Do your homework—research the company. Rather than a cover letter, write a well-crafted, specific email saying why you're interested in this job and what you feel you bring to that role. If you have some kind of transferable skill that may not be highlighted in a resume, talk about that and say here's why I think I'd be a great fit for your organization.

If you've taken a career break, don't be apologetic about it. You've gained valuable life experience—an asset, not a liability. When a job opportunity presents itself, take it, even though it may not be your dream position. Keep in mind that the first offer you accept after a break won't be your last job, but it could be the right position for right now. You will build skills, familiarize yourself with commonly used or contemporary platforms and applications on the job which help with productivity and communication within an organization. Work begets work, and once you establish yourself you can use every opportunity as a stepping stone to the next job.

With so many resources available, people coming back from a career break are much more supported than they have been in the past. Take advantage of every resource in your immediate, (as well as online) community to network, get emotional support, and bridge any skill gaps that may have arisen during your break.

* * * *

In order to come back strong and supported, brainstorm some of the ways you can parlay transferable skills to the workplace. How do some of your life experiences make you a strong job candidate?

How to Come Back Strong after a Career Break

1. Do some research on the field where you'd like to find work. How can you "upskill" and segue back into that field? What skills/courses/tech would help you transition back into this field?

2. Find companies or programs like Mom Relaunch that can help guide you through the relaunching process and give you the experience you'll need to be successful in your field of choice. Spend some time vetting any program before signing up. Look for press and reviews.

3. Be committed and true to yourself on this journey. Treat your training program as seriously as you would any job.

GET YOUR STORY STRAIGHT

"Your past does not equal your future. Identify your problems, but give your power and energy to solutions."

~ Tony Robbins

I'VE ALWAYS LOVED learning about history. If you don't know where you are coming from, you can't know where you're going. Looking backwards provides you with insight and perspective.

The work of the book so far has been to assess where you are and how you got here. When you look back on the story of your life, have you been a strong protagonist? Have you been capable, able to take on exciting new challenges, and do amazing things? Or is your story limiting you? Holding you stagnant in a place where you cannot get to the next level? Is your story big, or are you shrinking back and grabbing some background? Are you stuck in a mold that you've outgrown? Are you living your best life? If not, why?

In this chapter we intend to hone the first "R" of our Tri-R methodology: Realize. Connect with your story. Write it down. Although you may feel this pursuit is self-indulgent, hang in there. This exercise is intended to empower. If you do it right, you'll realize narrative clarity and that clarity, along with the concomitant internal focus, will aid you in realizing what you want. Then I will help you author your future story. I want to get you from where you are now to where you would like to be.

It's time to get your story straight.

Act I: Take Stock

Take stock of your story. Do some writing. Attempt to answer the questions that follow. Allow these questions to inspire you as you recall your career journey up to this point:

- How did you start out?
- Did you pursue the interests you studied in school?
- How did the actuality of that career align with your idealized vision?
- What were your first impressions? Things you liked/didn't like.
- Did you feel you were cut out for this work?

- Was your next career move part of a trajectory, or was this a step in a new direction?
- Were you engaged in the work?
- Were you respected at your job?
- Were you surprised or disillusioned by the job?
- How do you spend your free time? Are there passions you would like to pursue professionally?
- Did you chase your dreams/follow your passions?
- If so, did obligations get in the way of you pursuing your passion?
- Did you give up some ambition for a more reliable income?
- What were some of the lessons and hard knocks you learned along the way?
- Were there humble moments?
- Did you ever let your ego get in your way? Part of your learning curve may be dealing with ego and learning to let go.

Chance Welton, founder and CEO of Beachwood Marketing LLC, and the Millionaire Middleman Agency Coaching Program, credits a great deal of his success to making mistakes, learning from those mistakes, and letting go of ego. When I asked him to elaborate, he said:

If you don't see your blind spots, then you keep making the same mistakes over and over again. My partner, Abdul, and I told ourselves that when we start our business, we're gonna be one-mistake learners. If you are that way, and you learn after every single mistake, then you can actually become successful. But for so long, in so many ways—in my relationships, and my finances, in my energy, in my productivity—I was poor in all of those areas, because my ego was getting in the way.

As you look at the timeline and the circumstances of your career choices, it's quite possible you made random choices, trying things out, or perhaps you followed a trajectory without ever checking in with yourself to see how you felt about the direction you were heading in.

As you take stock, note what you liked and what you didn't like. What felt like a fit and what did not feel like a fit. Think about why that is. Learning what you don't want can be very useful in getting clarity on the kind of experience you do want.

Think about the people and the things that are no longer serving you. Regardless of how much time you invested in a career, think about letting it go. When you start letting things go and closing some doors, that's when you open up space for new possibilities.

Think about the kind of lifestyle you led in your early years versus the kind of lifestyle you lead now. Contrast the present and the past with the life you intend to lead. If there were jobs that required a lot of travel, would those kinds of jobs appeal to you now, or would you prefer a job that aligns with a more settled-down lifestyle?

Observe the patterns.

As you run through the episodes and experiences in your professional life, create a personal highlight reel in your mind to crystallize when you were at your best. What are the patterns you observe? For example, maybe you were given a few opportunities to manage a project, and you really enjoyed liaising with different departments and bringing everyone together to accomplish great results. How can you build on those strengths and look for a position where you will be a project manager? Are there gaps you need to fill to get you to that place?

Act II: Act with Intention

A career crossroads can be an uncertain time, and for some, a scary time. It is also a time of exciting possibilities. If we were screenwriters writing a screenplay, Act II would be described as the elusive heart of the screenplay. Act II is a place for serious character development. When you think about the movie heroes that you love, you likely acknowledge that they are all flawed individuals. If they were perfect, they would be perfectly unrelatable.

For our purposes, let's think of Act II as the place where you find yourself right now. What issues did you identify in Act I that might play into your current situation? Now that you have a handle on what you did and didn't like about your various positions over the years, what have you learned about yourself? Did you fare poorly in certain jobs because they really were not the right fit for you? Did you turn in sub-par work because you were bored and disconnected?

The great news about realizing these kinds of things that you want to change is that having that awareness is the first step. Now that you know that your perspective can help you frame things differently, you can behave differently as well. You are the author of your own story, and you now have the power to rewrite it.

Recently, someone sent me a 2010 article from *Marie Claire* magazine, in which Justine Musk gives an expose on her failed marriage to Elon Musk and talks about the excitement of reinventing herself. She was inspired when she attended a reading of Eve Ensler's new play shortly after their divorce:

Women disappeared after some point in their thirties, and any female ambition other than looking beautiful, shopping, and overseeing the domestic realm became an inconvenience. Being in that audience, watching that staged reading, I felt myself reclaim the freedom to write my own life.

Try to connect with the kind of power Justine describes. Is there a way to work with the ingredients of your resume and create a unique, inspired offering? Perhaps you were a teacher and you burned out and you don't want to teach anymore because it's become too much of a grind. But you love coaching kids, and on the side ended up spending lunchtimes coaching kids on their personal statements for college applications. Perhaps you could become a writing coach and either start up a business with other people or be a freelance writing coach/career counselor. Your extensive teaching experience would put you way ahead of the competition in terms of impressive credentials. You might already have several testimonials of families whose kids you helped get into competitive colleges.

An example of someone who was able to achieve this clarity about her story and pivot successfully is Wendy Paris, speaker, and author of *Splitopia*. I asked Wendy about how she assessed what was working and what wasn't working, and how she managed to pivot to create new opportunities.

Journalism really collapsed. I knew I didn't want to do corporate communications; I didn't want to do PR. Part of what made me think I could do well as a ghostwriter was that when I was looking for someone to help edit my Splitopia book, I called several editors who were recommended and each one said she was too busy. I was shocked. If book doctors are this busy, well that was exciting, because journalists are not this busy!

Wendy ended up taking her talent and her affinity for collaboration and she became a ghostwriter. Then, during the pandemic, she started working toward a master's in social work. Wendy has been a freelance journalist and an editor at *Psychology Today*. Obtaining a professional credential will put her in a position to be an expert *and* an author and that will open up brand new career paths.

Act II is always an important part of the hero's journey. Act II is usually where the protagonist has obtained sufficient experience and skill. Act II is where the protagonist is finally prepared to overcome obstacles, and this will be true for you at this stage as well. When you assess your story so far, can you tell which obstacles were external, and which were internal? When you are reinventing yourself, dealing with your own internal obstacles can be the biggest challenge. You may worry about ageism. If you feel like your age is the elephant in the room, is it really? Or is your insecurity about your age the real problem? Of course, ageism is real, and it is an insidious facet of many different professions. However, the experience that comes with age is invaluable, and when you start to reframe your attitude about your age and start to discount it as a factor, you gain confidence, and you will project a more positive attitude. If you've accumulated experience and skills, tell the world you're accomplished, and you're damn proud of it!

Helen Dennis points out, in an article in the Daily News, that 82% of adults over the age of forty-five who make a career change were ultimately successful.[15] While many of us have a stereotypical image of entrepreneurs as twenty-eight-year-old guys, "the highest rate of entrepreneurial activity in the U.S. is among those fifty-five to sixty-four years, according to The Kauffman Index of Startup Activity. That's been the case for the past fifteen years."[16]

Act II inevitably segues into Act III. Act III is where you set things in motion so that your career will be sustainable for the next decade or so. Though you may not know exactly how to connect all the dots, don't get overwhelmed. Think about yourself as a kid entering college and choosing a major. You are simply stating an

---

15 https://www.payscale.com/career-news/2019/01/most-older-adults-who-want-to-change-careers-succeed

16 https://www.dailynews.com/2020/02/29/successful-aging-why-older-people-are-starting-new-businesses-and-succeeding/

interest. You're not locked in to committing to this field. You're just checking it out.

Another helpful device is to work backwards. When you envision the kind of lifestyle you want to live and the kind of work experience you want to have, start to plan how you can get there. You're not imagining here, you're visualizing. Think about the steps that the protagonist in your story would need to take to make progress toward your goals. Though you may have made some impulsive choices in the past, now you have a chance to be intentional, smart, and strategic with your next move.

The next few chapters will help you fully flesh out your secret sauce, in order to create an individualized blueprint for success. This all starts with acknowledging your journey and giving yourself the gift of taking the lessons you've learned with you. Start taking charge. Start creating a professional path that is both personally and financially rewarding.

* * * *

What makes taking charge of your story so empowering is the reality that how you see yourself in the world affects your ability to make intentional career moves. Rather than trying to make *yourself* fit a job, you can start to think about finding the right work that will be a natural fit for your talents. You can make choices that align with the way you would like to see yourself, and the kind of legacy you would like to leave behind.

Let's Write Your Story!

1. Summarize your current story: What struggles did you face? If you have overcome challenges, how did those episodes empower you? Did you follow a straight path? Was your path interrupted? How do you feel you have internalized your story?

2. In writing your narrative, how have you gained perspective on the past? How will you act differently in the future?

3. Flash forward to retirement. If you were reflecting on your career, what are three things you would like to be able to say you achieved?

CORE COMPETENCIES

"Always define what you want to do with your life and what you have to offer to the world, in terms of your favorite talents/gifts/skills-not in terms of a job title."

~ Richard Nelson Bolles

THIS QUOTE SPEAKS to me because if you want to have a fulfilling career, you should not be molding yourself to a job title, you should be seeking work that suits who you are. If you were a business, your core competencies would be the resources and capabilities that comprise the strategic advantages you offer. If you are to find meaningful work and succeed in any industry, you must define, cultivate, and exploit your core competencies.

When writing this section, I was inspired by the 1970 classic best-selling book *What Color Is Your Parachute?* by Richard Bolles. It has been revised every year and has sold millions of copies, but I am still impressed by the original and how relevant it still is today. I was fortunate enough to meet with Richard's son, Gary, who is focused on the future of work, learning, and the organization. I especially love the flower petal model, "that one piece of paper" which served as a tool for people to find their core competencies, how and where they excel, and what their transferable skills are. The flower petal is all about taking a self-inventory. As Gary says,

This is a great exercise. It helps with self-esteem, language, and narrative. It allows you to talk about your personal narrative, to authentically tell your story and then map it to the needs of the employer. You've got to know not just what you're good at, but also what you love doing. It's a competitive market and most of us don't have the slightest idea what the mappability or the transferability of our skills from one environment to another actually is.

The famous flower petal exercise[17] includes the following areas (petals) for people to fill in:

Petal #1 – Goal, Purpose, or Mission in Life

Petal #2 – Favorite Knowledges or Fields of Interest

Petal #3 – Favorite Transferable Skills

Petal #4 – Preferred Kinds of People to Work With

---

17 https://www.shortform.com/blog/what-color-is-your-parachute-flower-exercise/

Petal #5 — Favorite Working Conditions

Petal #6 — Preferred Salary Range

Petal #7 — Preferred Place(s) to Live

When evaluating your strengths, do some brainstorming and free association. Was there something you were always drawn to as a child? Something you just knew you were meant to do? Did you lose that thread somewhere along the line? Is there something that makes you feel good, something you get lost in? What are you passionate about? What assets/talents do you have? What have people complimented you on at various positions that you have had over the years? Are you good at conceptual strategizing? Are you a detailed person? Are you a creative writer, problem-solver, team builder? What knowledge base and skill set do you bring to the table? What competitive advantages do you have over other people?

If you have ever had a performance review, list the factors that your reviewer used during the assessment. Then dig a level deeper behind those factors and identify the competency that lies beneath. Not only will this help you zero in on your strengths, this will also help you identify jobs you will not be a fit for. After all, if you are trying to be all things to all people you will stretch yourself too thin and set yourself up for failure.

In my discussion with Naeem Zafar, a Berkley business school professor, he said that his core competency is that he knows how to teach in a simple, yet powerful way and he loves to travel, so one of his career goals is to become a traveling professor. He explained this in less than a minute. It was a great example of the clarity of the vision that he has for his work-life harmony.

I spoke with Jeff Gothelf, author of *Forever Employable: How to Stop Looking for Work and Let Your Next Job Find You*, about some of the things holding people back and keeping them from leveraging their expertise and launching a new career.

The number one issue I find is people don't believe that they have something valuable to share. They don't believe that their story is unique. They see the internet as saturated with content and have no idea what they could contribute that has not already been done. They don't believe that they've done anything remarkable. They haven't had any amazing accolades in their life, they haven't worked with celebrities. They don't see the uniqueness of their story; they don't see themselves as having a story.

As a consultant and speaker, Jeff often talks about how to assess your core value.

What's the problem that you help people solve? When you get down to the layer beneath the job titles and job requirements, what is the core value that you bring to an organization, or that you bring to the people that work with you? When you can do this well, you get into things like, 'I help make complicated things simple.' 'I explain technology to non techies,' 'I help companies scale from medium to large,' right? These are the things that you should be conveying to an employer in an interview, especially if you're rebooting a career.

Finding a situation where you are going to feel motivated to go to work every morning is part of being forever employable. If you're not motivated, what would challenge you and make you grow? These exercises will help you achieve clarity around who you are and what the right professional fit will look like.

There are a handful of assessment tests you can do online; StrengthsFinder[18] is an excellent example. It was first developed as a tool to measure talent, the intent being that instead of going through life trying to make up for what you lack, you can understand your strengths and play to them. After completing the assessment you'll have uncovered your top five strengths. Thirty-four different strength themes are divided into four domains:

---

18 https://www.gallup.com/cliftonstrengths/en/strengthsfinder.aspx

Strategic thinking

- Analytical
- Context
- Futuristic
- Ideation
- Input
- Intellection
- Learner
- Strategic

Influencing

- Activator
- Command
- Communication
- Competition
- Maximizer
- Self-Assurance
- Significance
- Woo

Relationship building

- Adaptability
- Connectedness
- Developer
- Empathy
- Harmony
- Includer
- Individualization
- Positivity
- Relator

Executing

- Achiever
- Arranger
- Belief
- Consistency
- Deliberative
- Discipline
- Focus
- Responsibility
- Restorative

Getting clear on your strengths and focusing on them on a daily basis allows you to not only engage in your work, but also obtain and maintain better professional relationships, make more informed career decisions, and have a much deeper connection to what drives you and makes you feel happy and successful.

In Part Two, in the *You as a Brand* chapter, we will build on the assessment of your core competencies and strategize blending those skills to create a unique offering that really sets you apart.

* * * *

When working on the questions for this section, think of Richard's flower—what transferable skills do you possess? Remember to evaluate your hard skills as well as key soft skills. These kinds of exercises are really helpful in the sense that they give you clarity and get you laser-focused on the work you are drawn to, and the unique skill set that you possess.

Let's Work on Your Core Competencies

1. Start working on the flower petal exercise. Keep these in mind: What kind of work makes you feel alive? Is there a way to leverage your skills and abilities to merge with your passion to carve out a career path that will be successful and fulfilling at the same time?
2. How can you ensure that no matter what happens in your industry you'll remain forever employable? As organizations seek to reduce costs, automate tasks, and increase efficiency, how do you plan to remain relevant?
3. How can you build on your core competencies to double-down on the value proposition you bring?

ALIGNMENT FRAMEWORK

"Success depends on constant communication and complete alignment."

~ Marc Benioff

YOU'VE BEGUN THE journey inward to examine your story and assess where you are in your life and career. This chapter flows naturally after the preceding chapters because truly, a combination of those things, along with the unique perspective, experience, and talent that you bring—*that* is your secret sauce.

Now, we're going to kick things up, leave philosophy behind and put a plan into gear. Marc Benioff is a visionary. He wanted

Salesforce, and all the teams within Salesforce to have a vision, to develop a framework designed to achieve that vision and check-in with the progress of the team goals. Most forward-thinking organizations implement some sort of a framework—whether it's V2MOM (Visions, Values, Methods, Obstacles, Measures) or SWOT (Strengths, Weaknesses, Opportunities, Threats) analysis or OKRs (Objectives and Key Results). These are intended to put techniques in place that analyze and optimize progress toward a goal. It's a way for teams to feel like one vehicle driving in one direction, together.

Why is it that we all think about planning for certain things like a business, a project, or a trip, but we seldom take time to strategically plan our lives? As an entrepreneur, I have always found these kinds of frameworks extremely helpful, and I often wonder why each and every one of us does not create our own personal work-life framework. It's a great way to develop a personal management process that allows you to get clear on your vision, to assess what obstacles you'll need to overcome in order to achieve your vision.

Today we are changing all of that! A great first step is to write a V2MOM for yourself. If there is another framework that you prefer, use the one you're familiar with. Check out www.alignment.io[19] for suggestions. Just make sure that the framework you use is equipped to manage objectives and measure results. SWOT is a tried-and-true analysis that many organizations have been using for decades to strategize their practices. For our purposes, remember that strengths and weaknesses are related to each individual – if you were a computer, let's say this is your operating system. Opportunities and threats commonly focus on the world around you. Opportunities are there, though you may not always be aware of them. These alignment frameworks are so helpful in the preliminary stages of decision making and can be re-used as tools for evaluating

---

19 www.alignment.io

your strategic position at varying stages in your career. Once your analysis is complete, you can start to put the whole picture together and identify what your strategic advantages are.

For the sake of simplicity, I will use V2MOM as an example. This chapter implements content from a Salesforce.com learning tool called Trailhead[20]. At the end of the chapter, I have included my own as an example of how you can take this corporate tool and personalize it.

What's so appealing to me about the V2MOM is that it encourages creativity, change, and empowerment. It's not meant to be a tome—in fact, it should all fit on one page. It is, in effect, a snapshot of where you are at this particular moment in time. V2MOM is a living document presenting a powerful overview—not only the "what" (Vision) but also the "why" (Values), "how" (Methods), "why not" (Obstacles), and "how much" (Measures). It will provide invaluable information that you will need going forward to chart a course for success.

I spoke to Julie Trell, Head of Muru-D, and SheEO Country Lead for Australia. Julie has had extensive experience using these frameworks professionally both at Salesforce and in her companies. Personally, she has come up with two different methods of alignment. The first one is AI. No, not artificial intelligence. She is referring to "applied improv."

Improv forces you to let go and learn how to be fluid. You also have to be in the present and practice active listening. It's a behavior check-in—you learn how to show up for yourself and for your partner/team. The second tool, of course, V2MOM is checking boxes and establishing quantifiable measurements, which is also so important. Having a framework that you create yourself keeps you honest with yourself. It's something that you can always check in with.

---

20   https://trailhead.salesforce.com/en/home

Breaking Down V2MOM

Vision: What Do You Want to Achieve?

The vision represents what you want to achieve or accomplish. It focuses on what's most important to you. Writing your vision helps you dig deep and articulate your desires. Paint a picture of what work-life harmony looks like for you.

I will never forget something I heard Marc Benioff say when I was considering specializing in Salesforce CRM technology. He said he wanted to make business applications as simple as buying books from Amazon. I loved this analogy because I absolutely related to the idea of a simple, intuitive platform, and the fact that he made it come alive had me completely sold.

Remember that in this exercise you are an individual. Think independently—where you work and who you work for. You're the only thing you're focused on here. Focus on yourself.

What is your bold vision for what you want to achieve this year? When writing about your vision, think about:

- What do you want to achieve?
- What impact will it have on your career, on your life, as well as on the people in your life and community?
- How can you make it inspiring, fun, and creative?

Julie spoke about a vision that crystalized for her in a dream:

A friend in London posted on Facebook that a connection of hers in Australia was looking for someone to fill her flip-flops and move to Australia and take over her position. That night, I actually dreamt I was living in Sydney—I really saw myself there, going for it and getting that job. It was a big risk, but I knew if I moved to Sydney, I would launch SheEO there just as I had launched it here. It was my subconscious steering me toward realizing that dream.

Values: What's Most Important to You?

Values represent the principles or beliefs that are most important as you pursue your vision. They guide everyday decisions and tradeoffs. Marc Benioff says that after making a list of values, he ranks them in order of importance. It's an exercise that forces him to choose between pairs of competing priorities — if everything is a priority, nothing is. For example, if you are in the middle of a crisis and you are concerned about your family's well-being, your V2MOM values might state:

- Safety
- Compassion
- Conservation
- Courage

All of the other things stem from safety, which is placed first in order of priorities.

Which values come to mind when thinking about the principles needed to achieve your vision? When writing about your values, consider:

- Which three values are most important as you pursue your vision?
- How can you articulate your values to show what it means to live them?
- How will these values guide your everyday decisions and tradeoffs?

Remember too, that as you look at companies where you'd like to work, you should also be trying to find out what their values are. I spoke to Gwendolyn Turner, Founder of Steele and Grace, about this.

On the company side, we always have to remember that people have a choice, right? More and more people are saying, does this company align with my values from a corporate social responsibility standpoint, and from a diversity standpoint.

Methods: The "How"

Methods represent the actions you take to achieve your vision.
    As you write your Methods:

- Keep it under 5 action items
- Rank these methods in order of priority
- Keep it simple and easy to follow

When Rebecca created her V2MOM a few months ago, she used one of the methods that we talk about in the Three-Legged-Stool chapter. She listed, "outsource laundry" under a method to achieve her goals. She found that by outsourcing her laundry to a reasonably inexpensive fluff and fold service she was able to eliminate trips up and down the stairs carrying heavy loads of laundry. She created more billable time in her day, and she was able to achieve a relatively neat home-work environment that did not have mounds of clothing on every chair that needed folding. She was thrilled with the results!

You may find as you craft the means to your end, some obstacles may occur, so let's talk about those.

Obstacles: What Is Preventing You from Being Successful?

Obstacles are things that block your progress, get in your way, or make it difficult to accomplish what you outlined. Identifying obstacles before you jump into your work helps you anticipate challenges and proactively consider how to overcome them.

When writing about obstacles, think about:

- Is this a real obstacle or a perceived obstacle?
- Are the obstacles internal, external, or both?
- Are you ready to overcome this obstacle on your own, or will you need help from other people?
- What challenges, problems, and issues are holding you back?

Two examples of obstacles Rebecca may have faced include:

No inexpensive laundry service nearby. Or all her laundry was shrinking and getting ruined, and she needed to find a better service.

Measures: How Do You Know You Have It?

Management thinker Peter Drucker is often quoted as saying, "You can't manage what you can't measure." You cannot know whether or not you are successful unless success is defined and tracked.

Measures keep you honest. They keep you true to yourself and your vision. I recently bought a HydroMATE motivation bottle after seeing Ashley Connell drinking from one. I knew I had to have this! It's a huge jug with time bars to hit during your day, keeping you accountable for drinking the recommended sixty-four ounces of water. Just buying the bottle and using it changed my behavior and gave me a measurable way of knowing I was hitting my hydration goal.

What are the barometers—the standards that can measure results for you? When you are figuring this out, focus on measurable outcomes of your work.

When writing about measures:

- How are your goals quantifiable?
- Recognize when you are in alignment and also when you are out of alignment with your goals, so you can make adjustments along the way
- Be specific, relevant, and timely
- Use numbers and data instead of broad statements
- Keep revising the numbers as you make progress
- Continue to challenge yourself if the numbers seem easily achievable

I am happy to include this V2MOM I created as an example. I have not shared it publicly before but doing so here makes me all the more accountable to myself and to everyone I told that I'd achieve these objectives!

Reena's V2MOM

Vision

To live a fun, fulfilled, and comfortable life, lived with intention.

Values

- Trust
- Be helpful & resourceful

- Results-oriented
- Nurturing and motivating
- Bold, risk-taking

Methods

- Set aside time to meditate and take walks (or other exercise) every day
- Enjoy little things and the small moments. Spend time with family and friends and my pooch Rocky
- Eliminate negative influences
- Offer support to family and friends who need me. Spread positive energy
- Manage my time effectively with a detailed personal calendar
- Read all the books on my to-read list
- Pay success forward, teach and mentor others
- Travel, have new experiences, and meet new people

Obstacles

- Overcommitting to too many projects
- Clean freak and perfectionist tendencies
- Getting tired and low on energy

Measures

- Feel happy and fulfilled on the happiness scale that I set for myself
- Check off tasks getting done

- People around me feel energized and enjoy my company
- Continue to celebrate every New Year's in a new place
- Financially comfortable
- Measure 3S — Seva (Service), Satsang (Good company), Sadhana (Self-care)

* * * *

Creating an alignment framework for yourself will pull everything from the first few chapters into place and help you achieve clarity. Once you have that clarity, you can communicate to yourself, and others, what your objectives are. The second section of the book will show you how to get there.

Create Your Alignment Framework

1. Pick a framework that appeals to you. Start working on it with a clear and calm mind. Your framework should be simple and achievable. Stick to bullet points.

2. Analyze how you will use your strengths to achieve your vision for work-life harmony. How will you work on addressing your weaknesses? How do you plan to be accountable and responsible to continue to be aligned with your framework?

3. Make a list of people who you can trust to give honest feedback. Ask them to help you review your framework.

SUCCESS VS. HAPPINESS

"Everyone wants to live on top of the mountain, but all the happiness and growth occurs while you're climbing it."

~ Andy Rooney

When Steve Jobs gave a commencement speech to the graduating class of Stanford in 2008, he talked about success. The lesson he learned from being fired from Apple at age thirty, (he would, of course, end up being asked back) in what was widely perceived as a very public failure, was that he still loved what he did.

I didn't see it then, but it turned out that getting fired from Apple was the best thing that could have ever happened to me. The heaviness of being successful was replaced by the lightness of being a beginner again, less sure about everything. It freed me to enter one of the most creative periods of my life.

I purposely chose to title this chapter, "Success vs. Happiness," because contrary to the idea of success and happiness going hand in hand, the two are regrettably too often in opposition.

Success is something that's much easier to define because it's more tangible. "Success" usually means the achievement of a goal, and the status that goes along with it. But as any Silicon Valley psychiatrist can tell you, obtaining these achievements, and attaining this status does not necessarily create a recipe for happiness.

Though many people define success monetarily, the definition of happiness is more abstract, and much harder to articulate. Happiness is a feeling, a feeling that cannot be measured in promotions, condos, or Teslas. A good example of success vs. happiness is the measure of success for a good teacher. A teacher is seldom teaching to become rich. He or she might measure success by asking the questions: Do I make a difference? Am I fulfilled? Have I achieved my goal of passing my knowledge on to these students?

In her autobiography, *Becoming,* Michelle Obama expressed the experience of discovering what made her truly happy professionally so eloquently that I was provoked immediately into recognition. She realized that while she had plodded along on an ambitious path she laid out as a teenager, checking every box—going to Princeton as an undergraduate, then Harvard Law School, landing the plum job as an associate at the prestigious law firm, one day she came to a real soul-searching moment. She knew in her heart that her high-powered, successful law career was not in alignment with who she was and what she truly hoped to achieve in this life. So, at the age of twenty-eight, she changed course. She left the corporate world for the nonprofit sector and she never looked back.

Since this is a book about work-life harmony, it is important that you get clear on how you define success. One of the most common ways our lives become unbalanced is when we prioritize work at the expense of everything else. Financial achievement is a great means to an end, but if it is indeed the end goal, it will be a hollow success. When Peter Lynch, a man *Time* once referred to as the number-one money manager in the world departed the Magellan Fund at age forty-six it was in hopes of achieving some balance in his life:

When you start to confuse Freddie Mac, Sallie Mae, and Fannie Mae with members of your family, and you remember two thousand stock symbols but forget the children's birthdays, there's a good chance you've become too wrapped up in your work.[21]

Let's examine success in the philosophical sense so that you can become clear on what is going to make you feel happy in life. And since happiness and success are definitely not one and the same, I'd like to share some interesting research that has been done in this area.

Jonathan Biggane, Ph.D. wrote a book called, *The Happiest People*[22]. Jonathan credits Sonja Lyubomirsky with influencing his field of study. Since the late '90s, Dr. Lyubomirsky, a certified pioneer, has studied happiness.[23]

---

21 Lynch, Peter, and John Rothchild. *Beating the Street*. Norwalk, CT: Easton Press, 1993.

22 https://www.amazon.com/Happiest-People-Understanding-Science-Happiness/dp/B087SGSSB8/ref=sr_1_1?dchild=1&keywords=the+happiest+people&qid=1600040559&sr=8-1

23 http://sonjalyubomirsky.com/

While discussing Dr. Lyubomirsky's findings that fifty percent of happiness is genetic, forty percent is behavioral, and ten percent is situational, Dr. Biggane pointed out something I thought was fascinating. He said, "Only ten percent of happiness is situational, but people think it's ninety percent, which is completely backward."

People get hung up on thoughts like, if I move to California, or, if I get this job or promotion, or, if I get this cooler car, I'll be happy. The idea that your happiness goes up exponentially from these superficial things is a misconception. So, rather than focusing on the ten percent, focus on the forty percent that is in your control. There may be things you can change, like your line of work, or your commute to work that actually make a big difference in your daily happiness. Many people get lost because they are pursuing the wrong things. We look at certain celebrities who "have it all" and wonder why they are not happy. It's because money matters, but only to a point. Once you have your basic needs met—meaning you're able to pay your bills and be comfortable—more money is not going to make you significantly happier. In fact, studies show that the richest people are only marginally happier than people with average incomes. Where we find money makes a difference is when we look at people with no money, or very little money, vs. people who are comfortable.

Dr. Biggane also talked about the hedonic treadmill, a concept I was not familiar with. The hedonic treadmill (also known as *hedonic adaptation*) is a theory positing that people repeatedly return to their baseline level of happiness, regardless of what happens to them. If we're constantly pursuing the wrong things, that target is going to continually be moving, and it will never be hit. We adapt to our circumstances, good or bad.

As you develop a framework for happiness, consider how you can work with the behavioral forty percent—the forty percent Dr.

Biggane says is within your control. Think about the following categories of behaviors and consider how they could improve your happiness.

Pick Your Currency

What will success look like to you in terms of achievements? What will success feel like? Perhaps you envision a busy life where you work hard and then slow down to travel the world. Perhaps you have children, and you want to be able to save enough money for their education and their future. Perhaps you have an elderly parent you want to care for.

If material things factor into your picture of success, ask yourself why you desire those things. If you want a house, is it because you're keeping up with the Joneses or is it because you picture yourself living there and enjoying that city, that town, that neighborhood? Is it because real estate is an investment that is important to you for some reason? Does it represent security for your family and your family's future? If you desire a second home, is it for status? Or is it an important means to escape and enjoy vacation time?

The Journey

When I am coaching clients who are considering an entrepreneurial path, I tell them that first and foremost they should be deeply committed to why they are doing this, and always refer back to that "why" because this road will be challenging. Then, I ask them to be prepared for the worst outcome. You can't let even the worst outcome drain you emotionally or financially or take your smile away. Whatever the outcome, if you think you can still walk out saying that this was a valuable journey and you had an opportunity for personal and professional growth, then you are on the right path.

According to Dr. Lyubomirsky, success can be a factor that contributes to one's happiness. Many studies indicate that happy people tend to be successful across multiple domains in life, including work performance, income, health, friendship, and even marriage.

Invest in Yourself

Believing in yourself is at the core of any success you will achieve. You must envision yourself achieving great things and take steps to make those dreams realities. Invest in your own spiritual, mental, and overall personal development. This can mean anything from committing to working with a career coach, taking self-improvement courses/webinars, or going for a degree you are passionate about. Buy a stack of inspiring books and read one a week. I am a huge fan of Tony Robbins, Melinda Gates, Ruth Bader Ginsberg, and Sri Sri Ravi Shankar, to name a few. It is important for you to affirm your belief in your abilities because the energy you put out will instill confidence in others.

Gratitude

It is important to be clear on the fact that gratitude is a choice, it is not a result. The word is derived from the Latin word *gratia*, which means grace, graciousness, or gratefulness (depending on the context). Many people think that we experience gratitude when things are going well and that gratitude is a result of those things, but a number of studies show that gratitude brings happiness—rather than the other way around. An article in Harvard Health[24] notes that, "In positive psychology research, gratitude is strongly and consistently associated with greater happiness. Gratitude helps people feel more positive emotions, relish good experiences, improve their health, deal with adversity, and build strong relationships."

Savoring is an important aspect of gratitude. It's tied in with the next category as well.

Live in the Moment

Yes, this phrase is overused, but since we are here for a finite period of time, living in the moment is an essential skill to master. It's important to honor the journey, no matter what phase of the journey you're currently on. Remain present. Whether you're struggling to make your dreams happen, or you're relatively successful by your own terms, or you're still striving for that success, you have to value your experiences and learn from them. If you're always focused on the next thing, and the next thing, you aren't really present—you're living in the future. Similarly, if you ruminate on mistakes and "what if's" you are also not present because you're living in the past.

Remove Toxins!

While I do not suggest that it's advisable to surround yourself with "yes men," I do believe that you should steer clear of toxic people and toxic situations. If you've identified a work situation that involves constantly being berated and belittled, take enough care of

---

24 https://www.health.harvard.edu/healthbeat/giving-thanks-can-make-you-happier

yourself to find a better situation. If there are toxic, negative, people in your life who tend to shoot down your ideas and spread negativity, you might want to reevaluate those relationships. If these are important people in your life, then you need to work through this issue with them. But if there is a "friend" or acquaintance in your life who continually attempts to make you feel bad about yourself, consider the Joy of Missing Out (JOMO) factor that could come from removing that person from your email list and the contacts in your phone. You will feel lighter. You will have made room in your life for more positive people. Congratulations.

Competitiveness

A certain level of competitiveness is healthy. However, continually comparing yourself to others is a dangerous path to travel. Recently I had an experience with a competitor who achieved something quite amazing. I read that an organization similar to Mom Relaunch, the company I founded, received substantial financial backing and celebrity endorsement. Perhaps, in my younger days, I might have been rattled by this and would have thought, *Why them and not me?* But when I read the article, I genuinely felt glad that the cause I have devoted a good deal of my time to is starting to gain momentum, and that my competitor's work is raising awareness. I actually emailed the founder, a woman I have become friendly with, to congratulate her on this impressive accomplishment. In my mind, the fact that they are getting a piece of the pie does not mean there is less pie for me. I believe there is enough pie to go around. Clearly, we are both doing great work, we are both lifting women up and creating career opportunities for them. Again, it comes back to the lesson I learned in my childhood: a rising tide lifts all boats. It is, indeed, true.

External and Internal Approval

Oftentimes, if you are working your way up you seek the approval of your superiors. When you seek promotions, try not to lose perspective, or lose sight of your long-term goals. Raises, promotion, and status are great, but truly feeling successful is an internal experience. It comes from a sense that your achievements are aligned with your values and your long-term goals.

Everyone has their own personal measuring-happiness-bar, and the same goes for success. For me, no one can tell me that I am successful. I am the only one who can do that. Success is when I have the strength to handle difficult situations with grace. Can I smile and create a positive atmosphere at work and at home? Do I have something left over at the end of the day to truly enjoy my family and be present for them? Are my kids happy? Are they following their passions? Am I an active member in my community, making a difference, and making an impact on someone's life? Only then do I know that I am successful.

Clearly, happiness and success have very little to do with luck. There may be an element of being in the right place at the right time, but these are happy accidents—not something you can plan. You have to actively participate in your own happiness. That active participation leads to a feeling of success. When you are doing something challenging that requires a skill you've honed, you get in a state of flow that creates happiness. What kind of work makes you feel alive? When you discover this, it's an amazing feeling.

* * * *

As you can see, on paper, the idea of success and happiness is not necessarily the same as what it might look like and feel like for you. It is a highly personal experience encompassing all the components of your personal and professional passions.

What Do Happiness and Success Look like and Feel like to You

1. Growing up, did you have a conception of happiness and success? Did you think they were one and the same? Think of a relative (or anyone who you knew and admired when you were young) and try to remember what it was that impressed you about that person.

2. Do people around you feel happy in your presence? If yes, ask them what qualities and characteristics you have that make them feel good when you are around. If not, then have the difficult conversations that might help you with a breakthrough. Do you have characteristics and tendencies that are stressing people out, making them feel uncomfortable, making them not want to be around you? This is important to understand because if you feel happy and successful, it reflects in your behavior and treatment of others.

3. Since we're emphasizing the journey and living in the moment, start a journal. This is a great way to ground you in the present, remember small moments and details, and collect information to refer to when you want to gauge what progress you've made toward your goals.

BALANCING YOUR THREE-LEGGED STOOL

"Most of us spend too much time on what is urgent and not enough time on what is important."

~ **Stephen R. Covey**

TO ROUND OUT the "Realize" section of the book I'd like to introduce you to the three-legged stool at the heart of our Tri-R Methodology (Realize, Reinvest, Relaunch). Now that we have delved into your story so far and started to do the work of realizing your core competencies and values, it's time to create a three-legged-stool of your own. One leg is friends and family, career is another leg, and wellness another. The concept is deeply personal and unique to each of us, but we should all develop a framework that can identify when our stool is out of balance and learn the strategies that can make it right again. Since this chapter is about priorities, it must be said that the main stool-balancing technique is proper time management.

This chapter is divided into two parts. The first part is an examination of priorities and desires on a more philosophical level—how do you see your wants and needs at this stage in your life? It is an assessment of your top-tier desires. I also want to raise awareness around taking control of what your priorities are. As Ted Capshaw, an executive coach who works in corporate leadership development so eloquently says to his clients: *Are you setting your priorities, or is someone else setting them for you?*

The second part of this chapter has to do with practical tips and insights—strategically walking that tightrope of work-life harmony. Here I will share my insights, explaining how you can optimize your productivity so you can work smarter. And most importantly, I will debunk the myth of multitasking and encourage you to remove that word from your vocabulary!

Clearly, for most people, work has morphed into a very different experience than it was for previous generations. Women are becoming a strong cornerstone of the workforce. Work is seldom left behind at the office, and now, especially because of the aftereffects of the global pandemic,more and more people will be working remotely.

Another factor that has slowly but surely challenged the possibility of work-life harmony has been the massive disruption of technology. Before laptops, cell phones, and the internet it was much more possible to have established boundaries between work and home. Now, not only is it more and more common to not have a traditional office setting, but it is also becoming less possible to leave work behind. Our phones ding, heralding emails, alerts and texts come in at all hours of the day and night. Boundaries are blurred, so while there is a good deal more freedom when you work remotely, there is also the danger of work taking over your life if you're not careful. The image of a workaholic used to be someone stuck at the office morning, noon, and night, but the modern workaholic is someone who is home working 24/7 and seldom present to interact with family and friends.

Another heavily weighted factor in lives becoming unbalanced is the corporate grind. Experiencing this pressure and dealing with a grueling schedule is a common experience for many people at a career crossroads. Are you chasing a high-powered career, or is it more of a compelling calling?

David Callahan, a highly respected voice in the world of culture, ethics, and philanthropy was our inspiration for this entire chapter. David is the founder and editor of *Inside Philanthropy*. Before launching *Inside Philanthropy* in 2014, David co-founded Demos, a national think tank. I asked David about his priorities—how they changed over the years, and how this impacted his career moves.

I had an awareness early on, say right after grad school, that I wanted to achieve balance in my life. I had a vision of a three-legged stool supported by one leg of professional success, one leg of family/relationships/friends, and one leg of health/fitness/physical well-being all balancing out. I knew I would not be happy if I went after one at the expense of the others.

I asked David if he prioritized different desires at different stages in his life, and since he has led a self-examined life, I wanted to know how he developed the framework that allows him to check in with his desires and determine if he was on track.

Absolutely. Earlier on I prioritized recognition, then financial security became more important when I had a family. I definitely knew I wanted to achieve some kind of impact—that was a steady influence in my thinking.

In my forties I really developed that framework, relating how my meta goals related to my professional life. After starting Demos and eventually growing to forty employees, I got to a place where I realized I was not enjoying myself. I didn't have enough recognition, financial compensation, or autonomy. It was around then that I decided to exit. Starting a family was probably the impetus that moved me toward a decision to pursue a different path and create my own opportunities, beyond Demos.

Originally, when I spoke with Ted Capshaw for the book, I thought we would include his thoughts on financial readiness, but something he said really struck me as a great example of proactively establishing your three-legged stool at the beginning of your career path, and always checking in with it. Ted said:

When my wife and I had children, I decided I was going to be at the bus stop every day at 3:00. I knew what I had to achieve financially—I was very intentional in setting up my coaching business so that the number of clients I needed to take on and the financial goals I needed to hit were all in service of my priority to have that hard end of the day at 3:00. My kids are now seven and eight, and I have stuck to that schedule to create the work-life balance that was so important to me.

When I think about my story, I too arranged my schedule so that I would be done at 3:00 p.m. when my kids got home from school. And though at the time I did not conceive of it in terms of David's three-legged stool analogy, I definitely had an awareness throughout the busiest years in my business to make time for my family, my health, and my work.

I spoke with Lauren Deen, author, and Emmy-award-winning TV producer, who juggled a very busy career and home life as the main breadwinner in her family. When I pointed out our career canvas and the concept of all of us having a framework to check in with a work-life harmony at the outset, and then at various points in a career path, she thought this would have been an immensely helpful resource to have had.

When I look back at all the jobs I had over the years, producing for Martha Stewart and then the different development jobs and executive producing jobs, I definitely feel like I was able to achieve more than anyone (including myself!) ever expected of me. That being said, I grabbed opportunities and ran with them, operating as more of an opportunist than a strategist. And I took my knocks. I had so much more stress and had so many more problems than was necessary. And maybe because the pressure was really on me to be the breadwinner, I took jobs that I didn't always want to take. There were times my life was definitely out of balance. I feel like if I had a tool like your career canvas to sort of thoughtfully create a blueprint, and then check in with it periodically, I could have steered my career more intentionally, rather than feeling like I'm on a crazy ride.

As we get into the hands-on, nuts-and-bolts section of discussing practical solutions to achieve work-life harmony, you should be aware that it's a great way to start thinking about merging your philosophical "top-tier" desires with the discipline to accomplish all that you need to get done in your day.

"Gee, how do you do it? How do you make it all work?"

Any successful woman who is raising children will find herself asked this question constantly. I learned not to let the question bother me—it was usually innocent—but I noted that only women get asked this question. There is often an implication that you must be shortchanging your family somehow if you are a successful businessperson.

Tina Fey addressed this very issue in her hilarious book, *Bossy Pants*. She also spoke about it in the New Yorker:

"How do you juggle it all?" people constantly ask me, with an accusatory look in their eyes. "You're screwing it all up, aren't you?" their eyes say. My standard answer is that I have the same struggles as any working parent but with the good fortune to be working at my dream job. Or sometimes I just hand them a juicy red apple I've poisoned in my working-mother witch cauldron and fly away.[25]

Ah, I do love Tina Fey. And I would add that these kinds of questions are a vicious cycle. Not only do they feed on the pressure that society puts on women, they also feed on the pressure that women put on themselves to be perfect. Gloria Steinem had it right when she said, "Superwoman is the adversary of the women's movement."

These Are My Three Golden Nuggets of Achieving That Work-Life Harmony

Over the years I have developed strategies that allowed me to achieve all that I wanted to achieve without throwing my life off balance. They have gotten me through the most demanding periods of my career—when I was scaling my company and running an international team while raising two small kids. This is how I focus, prioritize, and get all the things on my to-do list done on any given day.

---

[25] https://www.newyorker.com/magazine/2011/02/14/confessions-of-a-juggler

1. Time Management

Time is by far the most precious commodity we have. Your success and happiness depend on prioritizing values and mastering time management, because if you don't, your stool will definitely be off balance. Whether you work in a factory, drive rideshare, or run a multi-million-dollar company, we all have those twenty-four hours to work with—no more, and no less. However, there are ways to utilize those twenty-four hours so they feel more like forty-eight hours, but these ways require a conscious decision to break old habits and change your approach. These are the productivity hacks that changed my life and enabled me to achieve all that I wanted to achieve when I was running my business and raising a family.

Survival of the Focused

You may be wondering why I include focus under the category of time management. I actually consider it to be the most critical element in proper time management. And the critical element of mastering focus lies in eliminating "multitasking" from your vocabulary. Multitasking means your focus is all over the place. This is a terrible idea! If you are to achieve any of your goals, learning focus is the most important first step.

The key to focus is removing distractions, and creating a work zone, whether you're at home, at the office, or in a communal space. Those dinging phones, apps, and alerts must be silenced. Make friends with the Do Not Disturb mode on your phone. Noise-canceling headphones and other devices that help remove distractions are also great tools. You must have the discipline to not touch your phone unless it is an emergency. Email and social media are distractions that dilute your focus.

When I coach candidates, I explain in no uncertain terms: "When you are working on a task, that task is your priority." This is not to say that your kids are not a priority. What I mean is that at that moment, your priority is work. That way you can give your full attention to your work when you're working, and give your full, undiluted attention to your kids when you are with your kids. Nothing ever gets accomplished if you are thinking of something else while you are working on the task at hand.

For me, the magical zone I found was early mornings from 2:00 a.m. to 8:00 a.m. In the early days of running my business with a global team and clients, many of whom were in India, half a day ahead of me in Northern California, I found that when most people start their day I was about to end mine. By morning, I accomplished about ten to twelve hours of work, because I felt my productivity doubled in that time period. This ritual began for practical reasons, but I continued with it for over fifteen years because I was hell-bent on finishing my day by 3:00 p.m. when my kids got home from school.

The main thing is, whether you're an "early bird gets the worm" type or a night owl, find that stolen time when you can cut out all distractions. Find the physical and mental space to focus. Make a habit of getting into your zone.

Scheduling

Everyone in my family was groomed early on to handle time management using the family calendar. By having a work calendar and a family calendar I slotted time for every single thing, making sure that wellness—meditation, walks, and exercise—were squeezed into my day. As David Callahan so wisely noted in his three-legged stool analogy, if your health is not a priority, your stool is going to be out of balance. I believe strongly in a practice of meditation, and also a practice of taking time to feel grateful and appreciate the gifts that I have in my life. My calendar has reminders for everything, even my own birthday, so I don't toil away into the night and forget to celebrate myself!

Documentation

My family is used to my exhaustive Google docs that I use to document and strategize everything from family trips, party planning, all the way to my son's graduation. It's a way of taking a strategic business habit and implementing it in your life. These documents can help you organize tasks and manage your time effectively. Sharing them with people ensures all the collaborators are on the same page. This saves time, often eliminating multiple emails and dozens of phone calls.

JOMO

The Joy of Missing Out (JOMO) addresses the black hole of lost time on social media. Most of us are connected through social media. We post, we comment, we partake in groups and chats on Facebook, Instagram, and WhatsApp. This involvement can be anything from a once-weekly check-in to an all-day-long obsession. Some of it comes from a genuine desire to connect with friends and family but beware the FOMO element of constantly needing to see and be seen for fear of missing out on something. Consider, instead the JOMO. Imagine the time and focus you can apply to achieving your dreams if you focus on yourself and make these goals a priority. Try it for a few weeks and see all that you can accomplish when you go "dark."

2. Working Remotely

According to Forbes Magazine, "When you dive into remote work statistics, you will find that in countries like the U.S., there's a 159%

increase in people who are working remotely from 2005 to 2017. Remote working jobs are no longer customer service jobs. They are in sectors such as Computer and IT, Medical and Health, Sales and Education as well. According to the American Psychological Association, there's also an increase in job satisfaction while working remotely."[26]

Obviously much has changed since the 2020 global pandemic. The lockdown was a massive disruption on the work front, and it is becoming clear that a sizable shift is happening regarding how people will work going forward. A 2019 study done in England shows a high demand for flexible working, with statistics indicating that:

- 81% of employees feel that flexible working makes a job more attractive to them.
- 79% believe flexible working would make them more productive.
- 92% of millennials identify flexibility as a top priority when job hunting.
- 35% of employees would prefer flexible working rather than a pay raise.
- 80% of women want flexibility in their next role.
- 52% of men want flexibility in their next role.[27]

When I started my first business, Avankia, I also had a baby. I found by working at home I was able to be flexible, and that flexibility allowed me to manage my work-life harmony. I felt a sense of control that helped me focus and be more productive. I was able to start and end my day when I chose. If I needed to accommodate errands, doctor's appointments, school schedules, etc., I had the flexibility

---

26   https://www.apa.org/monitor/2019/10/cover-remote-work
27   https://capabilityjane.com/about-us/flexible-working/

to do that. When I took a break from work I could start a load of laundry, and then switch the laundry on my next break so that when I got home I didn't face another hour or two of housework.

Apart from allowing a home-life balance, there are several additional reasons why remote work can be a boon to employees and employers alike. These include less commute stress, money saved on gas, auto maintenance, train tickets, etc.

Location Independence

If you are not commuting to the office, this opens up possibilities for operating from anywhere where you have good internet. You do not necessarily have to plan your life around living in a major metropolitan area. Military spouses who are stranded on a base could be focusing on their own careers by working remotely. It opens up so many different possibilities for people.

Employers Can Have a Broader, More Diverse Reach of Candidates

If the trend of increased remote working continues, employers can seek people out from all over the country and in fact, there are more and more businesses that have international remote teams.

Saving Money

Remote working saves employees money on expenses like commuting and dry cleaning.

According to Global Workplace Analytics[28], a typical company can save around $11,000 per year for every employee who works

---

[28] https://globalworkplaceanalytics.com/work-at-home-after-covid-19-our-forecast

from home at least some of the time. The areas that can save businesses money include rent and utilities, cleaning services, food, and taxes.

Health Benefits

There are studies indicating that overall workplace stress is greatly reduced by working remotely. An article in Forbes notes that out of the three thousand workers surveyed[29] by FlexJobs, 77% responded that they would be healthier if they had a flexible job and 86% said that they would be less stressed.

Climate Benefits

When lockdown orders happened during the COVID-19 pandemic, many people in places like Los Angeles—plagued by smog on a typical day—noticed cleaner looking and smelling air than they had experienced in decades. When you remove millions of cars from the road and reduce air travel, the environment responds almost overnight.

3. Outsource It

You will find that when it comes to raising kids, maintaining a spotless home, shopping, cooking, cleaning, and running a full-time business—something's got to give. Prioritize what you need to do and what you can outsource. This goes for home and work, and if you work at home, it is even more essential you set boundaries. If you need to achieve everything on your list in one day you may need to outsource things that other people can handle. On

---

29 https://www.flexjobs.com/blog/post/2018-annual-survey-finds-workers-more-productive-at-home/

the domestic side, this can be anything from help with childcare, housework, shopping, cooking, paying bills. If I make a meal, I make sure to cook in large batches and freeze future meals. From the time they were little, my kids knew they were responsible for making their beds, and keeping their rooms organized. This is not to say that *Good Housekeeping* featured us in a spread—there were days the kids' rooms were a disaster, and we had to stay on top of them to pick up after themselves.

On the professional side, this may look like hiring staff to help with administrative and accounting, and on up to PR, social media, scheduling, and travel. When I ran staffing companies, I was very cognizant of people's lives outside of work. We had a very family-friendly culture and we tried to ensure that employees got a day off on their birthday or their anniversary.

It was a nice feeling to know that I was supporting a small ecosystem in a way by outsourcing and employing people to do jobs both inside and outside my home. For me it was a win-win—taking some stress off my plate, while allowing me to achieve what I needed to achieve and create jobs for other people.

It's important to note that while women struggle under the weight of this ridiculous concept of "having it all," men also have a great deal of pressure to be successful while endeavoring to achieve that perfect work-life balance as well. They are trying to be attentive husbands and parents who make it to all the performances, parent-teacher conferences, concerts, and sporting events without feeling like the absentee dad disappointing the family.

In the Friends, Family and Your Support System chapter, we will delve into deconstructing partnerships that work. Whether you and your partner both work, or one stays home for a period of time, it is critical to have a discussion before you have kids so that there is a roadmap for shared responsibilities.

* * * *

Now that you've taken time to take stock of your desires, these hands-on exercises in prioritization will get you to start thinking about balancing that work-life-health stool.

Set up Your Top-Tier Desires and Priorities

1. List your top 3 desires. Now, imagine you have achieved these things. How do you feel about it? Does it make you fulfilled and happy? Are your top-tier desires related to material possession or are they related to meaningful relationships and people? Take stock of a few of the most meaningful relationships you have. What can you do to strengthen these relationships?

2. Think about a manageable way to make time for your priorities. Work on an ideal schedule. What will that look like daily/weekly/monthly? Allot time slots. Determine whether these slots occur in the morning or evening. Allot 1 hour health, x hours work, 2 hours family/friends/cooking/eating, 1 hour media, etc. Make it fun—include video chats to connect with family and friends.

3. Now list the restrictions or roadblocks that are stopping you from following through on achieving these goals. How many of those are in your control? How many are not? How can you work on reducing the impact of the things that are in your control? How can you learn to accept the things that are not in your control?

CHECKLIST

In the introduction, we provided a personal workbook link for you to use. Please download the online workbook at the link in the footnote. You can also create a copy of it to use online.[30]

Before you proceed to the next section, make sure you have the following things in place:

1. How you got here – Evaluate your current situation, lessons learned, and what you can change going forward.

2. Your story – Write your story so far. Write how you would like your story to unfold going forward.

3. Core Competencies – Start thinking about how you are going to maximize your strengths and competencies to live the life you want.

4. Alignment Framework – Your own personal vision and how you can achieve it.

5. Success vs. Happiness – Pick your currency and work towards it. Understand that success and happiness may not go hand in hand, so find the things that make you happy.

PART TWO

REINVEST
PREPARE YOURSELF

When I was coming up with a title for the second section of our book, I originally called it Reinvent, until I took a cue from professional coach Ted Capshaw who suggested, instead, *Reinvest*. Reinventing connotes becoming someone new but *reinvesting* in your core is really much more on message with realizing your strengths and doubling down.

As we build an awareness of what your three-legged stool looks like, how will you reinvest in yourself to build on the realizations of the first section? Remember that lasagna analogy from the introduction? There is a baked-in layering effect happening here. When you take your secret sauce from section one and reinvest in yourself through networking, seeking mentors, being a lifelong learner, finding your professional ecosystem, then rounding it out with personal wellness, you will move beyond your career interruption and discover a path to come into your own both personally and professionally. Now you're cooking!

LIFELONG LEARNING

"Forget talent. If you have it, fine. Use it. If you don't have it, it doesn't matter. As habit is more dependable than inspiration, continued learning is more dependable than talent."

~ Octavia Butler

JUST AS WORK culture and technology evolve, there will also be a continual evolution of information you need to stay on top of in absolutely every industry if you want to be relevant in your field.

The good news is, now that you are leaning into your strengths, you will be naturally curious to know all there is to know about new developments in your field. Lifelong learning is about reinvesting in yourself by seeking knowledge and staying curious, not only in your career path but in life.

Reinvesting in yourself also means opening yourself up to new possibilities. To contextualize lifelong learning, consider these three facts:

- People are living longer, with global life expectancy projected to rise from 72.5 years in 2020 to 80 years in 2080.
- We are no longer living in an age where employees stay with a company for 40 years and then retire. According to Forbes, the average employee stays 4.6 years at a job.
- The landscape of work is ever evolving.

Consider these nine popular professions that did not exist twenty years ago:

- Podcaster and podcast producers
- Online career coach, (online writing coach, online business coach, health coach, etc.)
- Social media manager
- SEO specialist
- App developer
- Rideshare driver
- Instagram influencer
- Driverless car engineer
- Telemedicine physician

This opens up exciting opportunities that were not there for previous generations.

When you consider the advances in the last ten years in areas like biometrics, fintech, the force of social media impacting marketing, and just about every other field, and the current (and near future) implications of AI, just for starters, it's no secret that if companies don't continually innovate they will die out, like dinosaurs.

And while almost everyone understands that concept, how many of us have the same objective understanding about our own career? We get in a comfort zone and set the cruise control, denying the reality outside our door. In this highly competitive world where traditional models are continually disrupted (think of what Airbnb did to hotels, or Uber to taxis, or the internet to travel agencies), arming yourself with knowledge, and the ability to be agile are the key elements to ensure your survival. If you are afraid to step outside your comfort zone, or your ego prevents you from adapting as your industry evolves, you will get left behind.

Not only is work changing, but the way people work is evolving as well. It is increasingly common for people to diversify by working in more than one profession. For example, you might be a psychologist who is also an author and blogger. Or you might be a nutritionist who is also a public speaker and online wellness coach.

Starting with the first chapter of this book, we have been layering on the concepts of connecting to your core competencies and choosing a path that resonates not only with your strengths and values, but that thing—whatever it may be—that makes you feel alive.

With the kind of philosophical perspective one acquires after receiving a pancreatic cancer diagnosis, Steve Jobs, in that famous Stanford address he gave, was adamant about pursuing your passions. He told these students going off into the world to stay hungry and stay foolish. This hit home for me. If I were to choose the most critical, the most pivotal moment in my career, it was in 2005 when I decided to check out this thing called Salesforce that my client bought, which I had no idea how to use. I decided to devote my time to learning Salesforce because I was hungry and foolish enough to step out into the unknown. It is often these kinds of moves, whether you are following your intuition, your curiosity, or your passion, that pay back the biggest rewards in life.

If you have chosen a career you are passionate about, staying competitive and marketable will be second nature to you. If you are continuously improving and evaluating yourself by doing workshops, attending masterminds, listening to podcasts, reading blogs and newsletters from thought leaders you admire in the industry, and perhaps doing some writing and public speaking of your own, you will be continually adding value to your offering.

One area that has exploded in the last ten years is online learning. Enrollment is up in online universities, and traditional schools continue to add more options for online classes. With dozens of open online course providers, you can study machine learning, data science, digital marketing, video production, how to become a financial analyst, or choose from over 150,000 other classes! In Masterclass you can study art and creativity with Jeff Koons, voice acting with Nancy Cartwright, restaurant recipes at home with Gordon Ramsey, or take a screenwriting course from Aaron Sorkin. Learning is becoming less of a long-term commitment and more of something consumed in small bites.

Keeping pace with innovation is not just on the minds of employees and job seekers, it is also on the minds of anyone who owns or helps run a business. And the learning that's encouraged is not just centered around technology, it's about encouraging a culture of learning that enhances employees' ability to provide value for the customer.

Squarespace, a website creation platform, is a great example of a company that creates a learning culture where employees learn new skills perpetually. Jason O'Neill, Director of Learning and Development at Squarespace talks about the benefits of this kind of work culture. He says, "Research shows that great talent will be both drawn to and stay at companies that invest in employee development. This is intuitive and makes sense. Each one of us feels fulfilled and motivated when we are growing and measuring forward progress toward our individual purpose." [31]

At Mom Relaunch, we encourage a passion for learning, because being excited about innovation in your industry is a big part of creating work-life harmony. When you're passionate about the work you do, you feel more aligned with your values. You're continually banking new skills and knowledge that you can either use in your current position or take with you wherever you go.

David Blake, CEO of Degreed, an innovative online platform devoted to the expertise economy and co-author of *The Expertise Economy* talks about the importance of how companies use learning to engage and compete and why they like to hire people who, along with being talented, are also learners. The concept for Degreed was inspired by the question, "Tell me about your education." I spoke with David and asked him about the seeds of writing this book and starting his company.

If you ask people about their education, they will tell you where they went to university or what degree they have. Which, in many ways, is an absurdity. If I were to ask you, tell me about your health, and you said, 'Well, you know, I ran a marathon seventeen years ago.' We both know, that's an irrelevant response! So that was the genesis of Degreed. We needed the ability to reflect a lifetime of education, academic, professional training, and formal learning.

David also spoke about the concept of a skills gap, as a macroeconomic term.

The old model is just getting a master's degree and using it as a springboard into a new career. It's rarely very intentional to develop particular skills. But you can be much faster, more efficient, that much more

---

[31] https://www.themuse.com/advice/director-learning-development-squarespace-jason-oneill

economic if you begin to frame your career objectives in terms of skills and closing skill gaps.

This mentality makes the daunting idea of spending a whopping six figures to attend certain private master's programs seem a lot less appealing than creating a compelling skillset with a list of masterminds you've taken part in, or from taking courses offered by a well-known expert in your field.

Bearing the balanced stool in mind, in addition to sharpening skills and learning in your targeted profession, it's also important to remember the importance of reading. It has often been reported that Warren Buffett spends five to six hours per day reading newspapers, corporate reports, and books. Bill Gates reads fifty books per year. In a 2016 *New York Times* interview, he said, "Reading is still the main way that I both learn new things and test my understanding." This really resonated for both Rebecca and me. Several times a day one of us is either calling or pinging the other to talk about a podcast or a movie we discovered or sharing a link to an audiobook or an interesting article.

The power of reading is not just applicable to newspapers, self-help, and how-to books. You can leverage the power of reading by reading fiction. When Oprah was asked how much she makes from each book she recommends in her book club, she said that she makes no profit. When a friend asked incredulously what she is doing this book club for, she said that she loves books and the community that's created when people share them. "In my eyes, that was never what the book club was about," she said. "For me, the reward has always been the way your mind is expanded when you're exposed to new adventures and ideas. And what the writer Andre Dubus III calls 'the sacred connection between readers and characters.'"[32]

---

[32] https://www.oprahdaily.com/life/a25777945/oprah-power-of-book-club/

And if you are still wondering if lifelong learning is good for you, an article by Jeff Haden in *Inc.* magazine about a ninety-five-year Stanford study reveals one secret to living a longer, more fulfilling life. And the secret isn't living an easy, stress-free existence—it's working toward achieving a goal that makes you happier and live a longer life. So, in the words of Jeff Hader, "There's only one longitudinal study that truly matters. **Yours.** Make sure you're delighted with the results of *that* study."[33]

* * * *

With all the expanded possibilities for growing your knowledge base, coupled with the culture of learning encouraged by employers, it's an exciting time to sharpen your skills and add new qualifications to your resume. There's never been a better time to be hungry and foolish!

Are You Ready to Make Learning a Habit?

1. Have you invested time and energy into professional development? What are you doing to remain relevant? Have you identified any skills gaps that you need to fill in order to achieve your goals?
2. How does your learning align with your framework? If it is not aligned, then how can you create a learning path that can help you reach your vision?
3. How do you track your progress? Do you add learning accomplishments to your profile and social media?

---

33 https://www.inc.com/jeff-haden/this-95-year-stanford-study-reveals-1-secret-to-living-a-longer-more-fulfilling-life.html

MENTOR, COACH, GURU, GUIDE

"Show me a successful individual and I'll show you someone who had real positive influences in his or her life. I don't care what you do for a living—if you do it well I'm sure there was someone cheering you on or showing you the way. A mentor. I've had that push in my life, going back as far as I can remember."

~ Denzel Washington

PART OF SUCCEEDING is learning and being open to any and every resource that you can possibly utilize to gain knowledge that will help you forge a path to your goals. This can be a bible like *What Color is My Parachute?, Lean In,* or *Career Interrupted.* It can also be a guru or a mentor. There is a world of inspiration, wisdom, and encouragement to be had from mentors. And in turn, most people who have taken mentees under their wing feel that they've had a great experience being able to help someone in such a concrete, measurable way.

When I was first starting out as a woman entrepreneur in tech in this country, I had some inspirational advice that stuck with me throughout my career. It came at a time when I was at a crossroads, and I felt intimidated, not sure if I had what it took to make it. I remember being at an event with David Condra, who was the President of the Nashville Technology Council, and looking around.

"David, I am a brown-faced woman in a sea of white men. How can I compete?"

"*Look around the room,*" David said. "*Do you see anyone here who looks like you?*"

I had to answer no.

"*Exactly! You stand out. You are memorable. Lean on your difference and always be proud of where you came from and remember what you are capable of.*" I digested his advice and internalized it. I was not going to let anyone's opinion of me limit my capabilities in any way. I wore that advice like armor, and anytime I entered a room where I was the only woman, and a woman of color at that, David's words in my heart gave me strength.

It's undeniable that the business world can sometimes seem like a cold, competitive, place but remember that there are people out there who are more than willing to help nurture you along your career path. You just have to be intentional about finding the right kind of help from the right mentor.

I was fortunate enough to find powerful mentors at different stages in my career. Interestingly enough, though I originally felt intimidated by that sea of white men, many of my lifelong mentors have, in fact, been white men. One of the uncomfortable topics that I think society would benefit from discussing more is awareness of unconscious bias. This isn't just bias toward you; this is also bias you may feel toward someone else simply because of some imprint in your brain that separates you from them according to skin color or ethnicity. It's something everyone needs to acknowledge before we can move past it.

For this chapter, I had an opportunity to sit down with Dr. Shirley Davis, author, and global workforce expert. I asked her about how people can claim their power and build a strong network.

When you know who you are and play to your own strengths, it's also great to have a strong support network—your own personal board of advisors. I always want to be around people who are smarter than me, more successful than me, been there and done that, because they will help me to get there as well.

In her book, *The Seat*, Dr. Davis talked about strategies to get yourself a seat at the table, because even though you may have earned a seat, you may not be recognized, for whatever reason.[34] She also talks about using informal mentors, whether virtual mentors or just figures she looked up to. By observing them, listening

---

[34] https://drshirleydavis.com/tag/the-seat/

to their advice, and attending their sessions, she was able to emulate their success.

Let's take a closer look at the what, who, and how of mentoring. As with any methodology, there is no one way to do this—no right or wrong way—but this chapter can serve as a framework for you to start utilizing every connection available to you in your immediate village, as well as the vast resources available to you online.

What Is Mentoring?

So many relationships in business are transactional, but the first thing to remember about the definition of mentoring is that it is NOT transactional. Rather, it is a human connection—a reciprocal relationship. You should never enter any mentoring relationship without thinking about what you have to offer, even if it is just respect and gratitude.

For many people, when they think back on their most important mentor it is a teacher. I always loved the classic *Peanuts* comic where Peppermint Patty and Charlie Brown are leaning on a tree and she muses, "I wonder what teachers make?" Charlie Brown, the round-faced philosopher answers back, "A difference, Peppermint Patty, they make a difference!"

Mentors are reliable people in your life who not only show a genuine interest, they follow through. When I spoke with Kip Wright, President, and CEO of Genuent, an IT Staffing and Solutions provider about mentoring, he reinforced that point this way:

It's important as a mentor for you to be there throughout that person's journey. That mentor needs to be someone who's willing to be there with you through the whole process, to vent at times, and provide feedback, and be hard at times, and to always be really understanding and non-judgmental.

Who Should I Look to Mentor Me?

While working on this book, I called up my early mentor, David Condra, to tell him what a profound impact he made on my life, and after hearing this, he was filled with emotion. I guess I had never expressed just how much it meant to me to have him encourage me in that way, and when I did, all these years later, he was so touched.

Mentors are needed in different areas—we may refer to them as coach, advisor, mentor, guru, or guide. When I was at a particularly hectic moment in my life, both personally and professionally, I found a spiritual guru, Sri Sri Ravishankar, who had a huge impact on me. His sutras (wisdom) coupled with amazing breathing techniques, yoga instruction, and spiritual guidance helped me keep my sanity during the craziest times of my life. Today I proudly say that my ability to practice being non-reactive, calm, and meditative is in large part due to studying with him and practicing his teachings.

Before you look for a mentor, it's important to get clear about what you need. What is it that you are trying to learn? What are your short-term and long-term goals?

Now think about who you know in your network. Do you know someone who knows someone? Start a comprehensive Google sheet to brainstorm possible contacts. Who is already familiar with your work? Could they be your mentor? Could they point you to someone who could mentor you? Keep in mind, a mentor can be someone at any level. Someone you admire, a former boss, someone you worked with, or someone you hope to work with. List different types of mentors, taking into consideration the kind of support you would like to have. You can have multiple mentors—some may become advisors. List five people for each category. If someone says no to mentoring you, you shouldn't take this personally. Keep in touch—he or she may be able to help you down the line.

Now, work on your approach. My early mentor, David Condra had this advice to impart on approaching someone for help:

Have a pitch that can get that person's attention pretty quickly. If someone approaches me and says, 'I'd like to buy you coffee,' or 'I'd like to have lunch,' or 'I just would like to get twenty minutes of your time,' or whatever, that's just so vague and so undefined. The chances that I can help or that we'll be a fit for what the person has in mind are not great. But if you can give me enough information and help me understand, it's much more likely that I'll go, 'Oh, well, that's interesting, I'd like to know more about what you think we can do here together.'

From the mentee end, Chance Welton spoke about how he found his mentor, Abdul, who would eventually become his business partner.

When I met Abdul, he had a six to seven-figure agency. He was part of a mastermind that I joined and we just kind of hit it off. I really looked up to him. We got along really well, kind of right out of the gate. He was the most successful person out of a mastermind that had three-thousand people. So, I just kind of kept saying, 'Okay, well, if I keep hanging out with the right people and I keep leveling up, like, eventually, that's going to become my life, right?' Your friends are your future.

How Does Mentoring Work Exactly?

Again, use this as inspiration, knowing that obviously there is no one set way to go about mentoring or being a mentee. Mentoring requires considerable motivation and commitment on both ends. If you are pursuing a mentor, be sure that when you contact someone you specify your goals, and state what the ask actually is. You should try to meet regularly, and send a calendar invite so it's official and neither one of you will forget.

Mentors are people you should seek out at every stage of your career. It probably won't be the same person, and it definitely will not be the same advice. Consider, for example, a student fresh out of college, someone considering switching careers, and someone returning from a long career break. These are unique situations requiring different kinds of mentoring.

When entering a mentoring relationship, both mentor and mentee should focus on mutually defined goals that advance a mentee's skills, abilities, or competencies. As a mentee, you should make an agenda for your meeting, and come prepared, ready to listen with an open, receiving mind. If there are specific tasks like a cover letter or resume that you need help with, or you are considering a change in profession, you can bring that up with them.

Oftentimes, you will have different mentors at different stages of your career. Lauren Deen spoke about seeking out a certain kind of influence that she needed:

At certain jobs, I always went for this mother-mentor figure. It was about trust, advice, and judgment. It was someone who had my back. I was lucky to somehow find those people.

I love that Lauren spoke of a mother mentor figure because even though she went on to have both male and female mentors, it was about finding people who were caring, nurturing, and there for her in some very challenging work environments.

In your role as mentee, always keep in mind how valuable your mentor's time is. Mentors sacrifice hours they could use to pursue their own career goals and spend them furthering your career goals, so bring your energy, curiosity, and appreciation. Even if you have an agenda, be open to hearing advice that your mentor has to share, whatever it is. If he or she recommends a book to you, read it and share your thoughts at your next session to show that you are eager to learn.

Masterminds and Peersdom

Mastermind is a term that has come into the professional lexicon in the last five years because the concept has exploded in popularity. Peersdom is lesser-known—it is a term my son Rohan coined in seventh grade when he was assigned a new Chinese student to mentor. While tutoring the new student history and English he realized that this boy had excellent grades in honors algebra, a subject Rohan was not doing so well in. Over the course of their first few months working together, Rohan discovered a mutually beneficial learning experience that inspired him so much he created a peer-learning program that took off at his school. He expanded his Peersdom program to a website to reach other kids, schools, and organizations out there who can benefit from the wisdom of their peers.

Similarly, a mastermind is usually an online support group that is a curated mix of people on a similar path working toward a similar goal. And though sharing peer wisdom is a big component of masterminds, probably the most important aspect is accountability. Your mastermind can be a formal or informal group, but you should agree on a common purpose to be committed to, should meet regularly, and should check in with each member to provide a framework for setting and achieving goals. This is a great place to bounce ideas off each other, share knowledge (podcasts, books, websites), and give and receive honest feedback.

It was great to hear so many inspiring stories, not just from people who benefited from being a mentee or a mentor, but also people like Chance and Abdul who ended up becoming partners. In the next chapter, we will dive into networking, which is also something mentors can help with. Kip also spoke on his role as a mentor and not only helping network for people but actually teaching them the skill of networking.

If you can, help him or her network. Make connections. In certain instances, I knew my job as a mentor was to do what I could to kind of reinforce that next step and then to call and say, 'Well, what went right, what went wrong? What do we need to do?'

From my own experience having had success as a woman in Silicon Valley, I find it very rewarding to guide others, share my knowledge, lead and teach and learn along the way—to pay it forward.

* * * *

Reflect on moments in your life when you either had a mentor or might have benefited from the right guidance to help you get through a particular juncture. If you know the feeling of getting a helping hand you can appreciate the importance of continuing to seek out different mentors at different stages of your career. Also, think about who you can help. Think about skills you bring to the table and ways you could nurture someone else in their career path.

Let's Work on Our "Give" and "Ask" Muscles

1. Create an online-shareable document and list areas where you need help. Check the workbook for a sample format to use. List all the people you would like to reach out to, separated into three categories: friends and allies, targeted asks, and aspirational "reach" contacts. Add columns for contacts who can help you get connected with the mentors you are seeking to add to your

circle. Add columns for ask and give. Remember we all have something to give back in this reciprocal relationship.

2. Craft message templates you can use to reach out to potential mentors. Make sure to customize each letter with a specific ask. You don't want to be generic or vague.

3. Take action. Actually reach out to them. Be prepared to have positive and negative responses from people in different categories. Be grateful for every acceptance. Try to learn from rejections. Delve into these to determine whether there is something you can improve on in your approach.

HOW TO NETWORK EFFECTIVELY

"Your Network is your Net Worth."

~ Tim Sanders

WHENEVER ANYONE ASKS me what my secret sauce for success is, I always give three pieces of advice:

1. Network
2. Network
3. Network

My way of summarizing stuff in threes has become sort of fun at home and in my professional circle.

Did you know that the majority of all jobs are filled via networking? A CNBC article cites research indicating that 70% of all jobs are not published publicly on job sites and as much as 80% of jobs are filled through personal and professional connections.[35] That's a pretty powerful statistic.

Networking is a skill, and like any other skill, if you are going to master it you must work at it. Sometimes it means stretching yourself outside your comfort zone. This chapter will provide you with a springboard to hone your skills and beef up your networking game.

Networking can be as simple as reaching out to friends, family members, former colleagues, and long shots—perhaps people you admire who you follow on social media—to help further your career goals. Use your social media to reach out to people. In 2020, I reached out to Rebecca Cullen on LinkedIn because I saw that she had expertise in writing books, and that began an exciting partnership that led to the creation of this book.

Today, more than ever, your network is one of the most valuable assets you can have. Don't confuse this with the "connections" you have on social media. I'm talking about the people in your life who you actually "connect" with personally and professionally who are willing to go the extra mile for you. It's extremely important to know the difference.

Culled from a few decades of experience, these are my *network, network, network* nuggets.

---

[35] https://www.cnbc.com/2019/12/27/how-to-get-a-job-often-comes-down-to-one-elite-personal-asset.html

When Is the Right Time to Network?

Networking will play a role in every aspect of your career, but it is especially critical when you are in-between jobs, just let go, or transitioning back into the workforce. I was excited to sit down and speak with Jen Sargeant, Chief Operating Officer at Wondery for her wisdom in the Entrepreneurial Journey chapter, and she also had valuable input on the importance of networking.

Have a lot of conversations—conversations to hear yourself say what you want to do, conversations to have people poke holes in what you think you want to do. In my case, I did not necessarily know a single person at Wondery. But I networked into two people who did know Wondery. And then they connected the dots. I actually had not even thought about podcasting as my next career. But I knew what I wanted out of my next move, and it was all through conversations that happened. I think people don't always realize that they have people around them that will help them.

Of course, social media is a key element of marketing, and LinkedIn is the standout site you should make sure you are using.

How to Network on Social Media like a Pro

When it comes to social media, you need to be a little bit of a stalker. (Though you probably do not want to do this in real life!)

LinkedIn

LinkedIn is one of the most powerful platforms for anyone in the professional realm, and just like any social media—there is a way to do this effectively if you familiarize yourself with the ins-and-outs of how things work.

Many people do not realize that when you send a connection request, you have the opportunity to send a personal message. Take it. When you're trying to get someone's business or add them into your network—and this is particularly true of high net-worth individuals—do the LinkedIn two-step. Which is to say, find a mutual connection in your network who is connected to the high-level person you want to connect with. If you reach out to your connection and ask if he or she is open to making that intro, you will hopefully now have a warm introduction and a foot in the door.

Julie Mason, a top LinkedIn Guru, and founder of LinkedSalesFormula.com recommends that once you make this important connection, nurture it by adding value. She calls it "opening an emotional bank account." One example of how to go about doing this would be a simple thank you note including a link to a LinkedIn article that you wrote that may be of interest to them. Don't send them to an unknown site like your personal blog, as they may not trust the link.

Something else you might consider is that you can send a voice message on the LinkedIn app, which is a great idea for a human touch. And then, going off the reservation, Julie sometimes uses direct mail techniques, such as sending a mug with a positive affirmation to a prospect. "Lumpy mail," as she calls it, gets past the executive assistant, and winds up on the prospect's desk, hopefully brightening her day and again, adding that personal, unexpected element that makes an impression.

When it comes to introducing people in your network, Wendy Paris pointed out that when you connect two people, you're actually strengthening your own network in the process. It's that "rising tide" phenomenon again.

Facebook

I've heard so many people brag about the number of friends/connections they have on Facebook but remember that there is an oversaturation of interests being plugged on all these platforms. Yes, it's important to have a social media presence when you are trying to promote yourself and be an influencer. It can also be of some value if you're looking to get advice and referrals for jobs and opportunities. But join or form a core group that you can have hangouts and discussions with informally without any agenda.

Instagram

Instagram is used more for marketing than networking. You can incite engagement with hashtags and even join a group chat — otherwise known as an Instagram Pod. Many people are using Instagram live or Facebook live as a way of delivering content, like an interactive summit or event for a program, service, or product you want to promote.

Twitter

Twitter allows access to important players in your industry who may be otherwise difficult to reach. In an article on her site, Ashley Stahl shares an example of how Twitter allows you access to important players in your industry who are perhaps otherwise pretty impossible to reach.

"When my client Kaela told me about how badly she wanted to write for one a particular publication, I asked her what steps she had taken in order to pitch her articles.

Kaela had submitted her piece through the site's submission form and had followed up several times without hearing anything back. When I asked if she followed the editor of the section that she was looking to write for on Twitter, it had never dawned on her that she might be able to use social media for something like that." [36]

Ultimately Kaela not only got a shot, but her piece was one of the top performing articles of the month. Even the Editor-in-Chief retweeted it.

If you want to put yourself out there as a results leader, tweeting is a great avenue to do so. Because you only get 280 characters, you can become quotable with some of the snippets you post.

Hone Your Virtual Networking Skills

Networking in a virtual call is such an important skill to learn. It involves nuance and a bit of audacity. Because you are challenged by not being able to meet in person, you need to figure out ways to make an impression on whoever it is that you are meeting with. I've been fortunate enough to have honed this skill since 2002 when I decided to run my companies working from home. It is important to look in the camera when you talk and give all your focus and attention. If you are planning to take notes, consider recording the call on the computer or your phone instead so you don't appear distracted each time you look down to write. Apart from that, conduct yourself as though it was an in-person meeting.

My own style of networking is something Rebecca refers to as chutzpah! I reached out to the most impressive people I wanted to meet and interview for the book, figuring if they say no, they say no. Nothing ventured, nothing gained. So, when I reached out to Stu Heinecke, *Wall Street Journal* cartoonist and author of *How to Get a Meeting with Anyone* and he said, "Yes," I was very excited. Named the "father of contact marketing" by the American

---

[36] https://ashleystahl.com/how-to-network-on-twitter-without-looking-like-a-creep/

Marketing Association, Stu's mission is to provide unfair advantages to help enterprise/SMB/startup sales teams get more C-level meetings with top accounts faster and more effectively.

Profile scraping

If you're trying to get a meeting with someone, do some sleuthing. Stu refers to this as profile scraping. Find out more about the person you're trying to meet with. What do they like, what are their hobbies, what are they known for? Stu tells the story of an executive no one had been able to reach, and how, a new hire did some sleuthing and found out that this executive was interested in technology and had a passion for barbecuing.

The new guy on the team bought a barbecue apron and had it engraved with a Stanley C. Clarke quote: "Any sufficiently advanced technology is indistinguishable from magic." He sent this gift off, and not only did he get through right away, but he also landed a huge deal. Of course, the whole office wanted to know his secret.

Working the Room

Networking events are an excellent opportunity to have face-to-face interactions and establish new connections. Before I go to an event, I make a point to read every speaker's profile and connect with them on LinkedIn so that I can introduce myself at the event with some context. I bring a stack of business cards to hand out with my website, phone number, and that personalized LinkedIn Url on them. If I know the organizers of the event and there is someone I'm eager to meet, I will see if the organizer can connect us before the night is over.

Work Out Your Elevator Pitch for Your Ask

My mentor, David Condra, referenced the elevator pitch when I spoke with him. He mentioned it in the context of approaching an investor or mentor, but the concept is really applicable to so many situations, and if nothing else, it's a great exercise for you. It will help you get clarity on your value proposition.

An elevator pitch is something you can just state simply, say, in the space of a minute or two, that will help someone understand where you are, where you want to go, and whether they can bring something to that relationship that is of value or not, and whether you have something of interest to them.

What's in a Thank-You Note?

Everything!

Showing gratitude to the people in your network is extremely important. It may be just a simple thank you email, voicemail, or a card, but those two words go a long way. Be grateful for the knowledge and input of others, and their willingness to share it. If you just had an interview, by all means, follow up with a warm note expressing how much you enjoyed sitting down and talking with that person, and how you appreciate their time.

Snail-Mail Notes and Gifts

If you're in a Zoom meeting, take notes on what you think the person might be into. When I met with Stu, I was sitting out by my pool. He noticed:

I would send you a pool toy! Or a handwritten card. I send cards for all kinds of occasions, even when I want to ping someone to ask why he or she is not calling me back.

CAO (Chief Access Officer)

People often ask how to circumvent the assistants and the answer to that one is no! Don't do it. Executive assistants are some of the smartest, sharpest people in the company. I asked Stu to elaborate on this point:

Executive assistants probably have more influence and interaction with the CEO than anyone. So, I tell people, think of them as VPs of access, perhaps, Chief Access Officer. I think of them as talent scouts and get to know them because they speak right into the ear of the person I need to get my message to.

VIP Statement

Stu is someone who, (like me) also has a lot of chutzpah. He has done a great deal of outside-the-box thinking, which has resulted in some very creative deliveries to executives he was trying to get a meeting with. He suggests crafting a VIP statement. In Stu's case, he has been known to contact the assistant of the person he wants a meeting with. The VIP statement is something he prepares ahead of time to get that person's attention.

You need something that encapsulates the value that you hope to convey really quickly. Ideally, it's just a sentence or two. The idea is to do something, make some kind of gesture (like with the barbecue apron) that makes them say, hey, this is exactly the kind of audacity and ingenuity we need around here!

At the end of our talk, Stu emphasized:

Everything we do, every good thing that happens in our lives, happens because we make a connection with someone.

* * * *

Tell me the story of someone who has achieved a lot of success in her career, and I will show you someone who is good at leveraging her network. Think about all the ways you can step up your networking efforts both virtually and in-person to take your career to the next level.

Let's Explore Networking

1. What networking platforms (in person or virtual) are you using and how active are you? What is your brand on social media? How often do people reach out to you for advice and help?
2. Using Stu as inspiration, what is an out-of-the-box way you might get the attention of someone you are trying to meet?
3. List three ideas that you learned from this chapter to implement in the next 30 days.

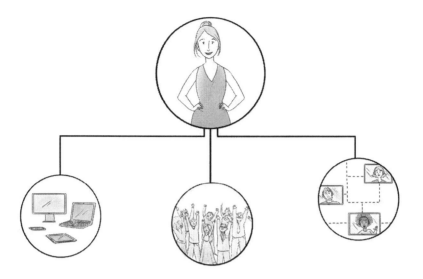

FIND YOUR PROFESSIONAL ECOSYSTEM

"Building and leveraging an ecosystem can have a flywheel effect on your career: the power of the network opens doors that you might not even know existed."

~ Avanish Sahai

THERE IS AN African proverb that says, *"If you want to go quickly, go alone. If you want to go far, go together."* An ecosystem is greater than the sum of its parts, so when you are part of a community, there is a huge upside in terms of personal and professional growth.

Nature is, of course, the inspiration for the ecosystem concept. In ecological terms, an ecosystem is a community of living organisms interacting with each other, breathing the same air, sharing the same water, mineral soil, and other elements. These organisms influence each other and their surroundings; they collaborate and compete, create and share resources, and adapt together to external disruptions.

You may be confused by the term professional ecosystem, a term very much in the zeitgeist that has some people scratching their heads, but the concept is not new. Think of a time (*before Amazon!*) where the bazaars in India or the market in Notting Hill brought buyers, sellers, and makers together in one communal forum. It is simply a communal environment where different individuals and companies with similar goals come together to collaborate, learn from each other, and grow along the way.

Part of the reason professional ecosystems are more and more in the spotlight is that the face of work has been disrupted by the internet. And that's a good thing! The traditional hierarchical structures are giving way to more innovative and creative collaborations. In this chapter, we will examine the many benefits of working and being part of an ecosystem where you can grow and thrive—to become part of something bigger that can lift you up and help fast-track your career success.

Some Examples of Professional Ecosystems to Leverage

Software

Ecosystems like Alibaba, AWS, Azure, Google, Intuit, Salesforce, and VMWare are some good examples to explore.

E-commerce

Etsy, eBay, Shopify, Amazon, Alibaba – These sites have taken people from selling a few items out of their garage to building substantial international businesses with their online shops.

Networking

Social Media platforms like Clubhouse and LinkedIn are great examples of an ecosystem you can use for networking, job hunting, self-promotion, and showcasing your work. Many writers on Medium join Facebook groups to seek advice, promote their work, and increase their expertise and their visibility. Upwork holds virtual and in-person seminars to help people learn how to better leverage the platform and create a strong profile.

Industry specialized groups – Being part of those groups not only helps with networking you also get to explore ideas and other issues others in your industry may be facing.

Increasing Exposure

If you are a writer or content creator, things have come a long way in the last decade. Rather than starting up your own blog and shouting in an empty room, you can create a blog on WordPress and take advantage of free SEO tools like YOAST, and start building a following using sites like Substack, Medium, Newsbreak, Facebook, YouTube, TikTok.

Human Cloud Platforms

If you'd like to explore your skills and earn some additional income as a writer, content creator, designer, software developer, proofreader, kindle formatter, or developmental editor, platforms like Upwork and Freelancer connect you with customers, handle billing and terms, and help you build up a profile and a clientele.

Online Coaching and Learning

Coaching and learning have blown up as a profession because suddenly there is a world of possibilities when it comes to reaching out to audiences, students, and clients. There are tutors, professors, and wellness coaches who have taken their business online and become much more successful than they would have if they opened a brick-and-mortar business. Doing business this way also eliminates commuting and the need for the overhead expenses of offices and staff. There are myriad platforms out there for teaching that handle your courses, digital downloads, customers, email subscribers, payments, and data all in one place.

I personally am a big believer in finding your ecosystem because my success would not have been possible without accidentally discovering this early on in my career. My companies were built around the professional ecosystem of Salesforce. I compare my situation to that of a little fish who (quite fortunately) attached herself to a big shark. Even though I call myself a solo, bootstrapped entrepreneur, I, in fact, had the support of billion-dollar company infrastructure. In my talks, I still use a slide showing headshots of all the CEOs of the companies that I was competing with. I was a brown-faced woman in a sea of white men remember? Many of those companies were well-funded, and at the time it was all very intimidating, but I am happy to say that I did not let this stop me.

Salesforce not only helped put me on the map, it also helped my company provide a better software solution because it was built on a more robust platform. Through all of the early stages of development, I always had the feeling with Salesforce that someone had my back. There is a collaborative and supportive environment that helped me achieve a much higher level of success much faster than I could have done on my own.

I met Mike Kreaden, managing director at Salesforce incubator, during the early days of working with Salesforce. He became a good friend and a true mentor for all my companies to date. He was instrumental in creating the Salesforce marketplace, called AppExchange, which they also refer to as application economy. He fondly recalls those days:

We felt that a key measure of success from an ecosystem perspective ultimately was going to be the number of partners, number of solutions, and the health of those partners. Could they create a line of business for Salesforce, let alone build a business on Salesforce?

Whatever industry you're in, whether it's business, IT, entertainment, journalism, or real estate, you have an ecosystem all around you that you need to connect with. Let's talk about the benefits you will get, as well as ways you can swim in your ecosystem and work with your network.

How to Find the Right Ecosystem?

Support

Depending on the industry you are in, the ecosystem should be able to bring the support you will need to scale you both professionally and personally. In my case, Salesforce offered the software infrastructure to build the products and also a marketplace to list and sell them. What else can you ask for as a small business owner?

Avanish Sahai, VP-ISV, and App partner ecosystem at Google summarizes it beautifully in one line:

I would say it's strength in numbers.

When I asked him to elaborate on picking the right ecosystem he said:

If you are deciding to specialize in a specific career track, then first evaluate how scarce and valuable those skills are and how to continue to build your career ladder in that ecosystem. Part of that is understanding where the industry is headed. And then aligning with what type of personal growth, technology growth, market opportunity, et cetera, that you're looking for.

Brand Association

Being part of the larger entity allows you to operate with a different status, which can bring a sense of pride. Rather than spending years doing the footwork involved in establishing your brand, you are automatically legitimized with the high awareness and authenticity of an established brand. Imagine your app is listed on Apple iTunes or Google Play store. That listing grants users instant access to search, download, give reviews, and pay.

The same concept applies if you are in retail and you become a seller on Amazon, or if you are a writer and you are getting exposure on platforms like Medium or LinkedIn. You gain instant credibility and trustworthiness by being aligned with these ecosystems, whereas on your own, this process could take years to establish.

A good place to start is to look for ecosystems that are established brands and have a substantial number of people.

When I reached out to Dr. Shirley Davis, to get her recommendation about joining the National Speakers Association, she responded enthusiastically.

I absolutely would recommend joining NSA. It's a wonderful organization for learning how to master your speaking ability AND for how to run a successful speaking and consulting firm.

Network Effect: Share and Learn from Each Other

Being part of an ecosystem is an unparalleled opportunity to expand your networking horizons. Learning from each other drives the product to constantly improve, and in turn, brings more customers and partners, and the cycle goes on.

Remember all the nuggets you learned in the networking chapter and apply them when you are working in your professional ecosystem. Networking done here can be amplified since there are mutual benefits and growth opportunities.

Avanish talked about this domino effect of positive effects:

It's like the learnings of each drive the product to be better, which drives people to come in which drives more learnings. And that cycle, I think, is something that is really important in an ecosystem, right? Because what you're trying to do as an ecosystem provider is to broaden the appeal and feed on each other's energy and enthusiasm.

Innovation

"Innovate or die" is something we often hear in regard to making it in business. Most of the ecosystems that are doing well are constantly innovating to meet the needs of everyone involved. When you are part of the ecosystem, think about what you are learning and how it is growing your career.

Avanish put this so well:

There is this feeling that for my personal growth, for my career growth, I'm going to learn new things. I'm going to either transform from where I was to this, or I'm gonna grow into this and continue to acquire new skills, new certifications, and new project areas by leveraging all the resources in the ecosystem.

Income Opportunities

Ecosystems can and should be used to create value. No single organization (or person) can create on his or her own. Look for opportunities where there is potential to grow your clientele and scale your income without hitting a dead end.

To use a simple analogy, if you decided to sell products online, you might be able to use the ecosystem of Alibaba or eBay, or utilize Amazon's ecosystem of sellers, buyers, advertisers, and collaborators to scale what you are doing. Having that kind of built-in infrastructure saves someone starting up a business a lot of time and money. There is no need to reinvent the wheel when you can hit the ground running.

Mike Kreaden talked about this dynamic in Salesforce:

They measured the success of the ecosystem based on the health of their partners, which includes how much income they are generating and how they can continue to grow and thrive. Every decision they made to innovate with and grow the ecosystem was to drive more revenue for everyone involved.

* * * *

I hope you're getting excited, seeing that ecosystems exist across all career avenues, opening up endless possibilities for finding an audience or pitching clientele for whatever niche you're interested in. Finding your ecosystem is a combination of pursuing opportunities to become a part of a larger system where you can achieve your goals while learning and continually innovating all while leveraging the support of a larger infrastructure. As I said, I was that little fish riding on the Salesforce shark, so find your shark who can help you navigate the waters of your chosen career.

Find Your Ecosystem Where You Fit In

1. Based on your area of interest, list some of the professional ecosystems that you can be part of and what role you can play there.

2. Chances are, there are online courses to teach you how to successfully utilize any professional ecosystem, whether it's Amazon, Medium, Upwork, etc. Look for the podcasts you can listen to and courses you can take that set you up for success on the path you are pursuing.

3. Since there is a lot of "noise" out there on the internet, if you choose to compete in a professional ecosystem, how will you distinguish yourself? How can you add substance and depth to your offering?

YOU AS A BRAND

"The only thing you take to your grave is your brand."

~ **Stephan Spencer**

WHAT IS THE first thought that comes to your mind when you think of the word brand? Most of us associate brands with companies, especially big ones that spend a lot of money creating impressions in the minds of the consumers they want to buy their product.

Zoom out for a moment to look at the historical context of all of this. According to an article in Fortune Magazine, more than 40% of America's baby boomers stayed with their employer for more than twenty years.[37] The work people did was to better the brand of the company for which they worked. And those companies, in return, took care of their workers with benefits like health insurance and 401k's.

But that was then. According to the Bureau of Labor Statistics, the median number of years that wage and salary workers have been with their current employer is 4.2 years.[38] There is more jumping around, more transition, and therefore, as we move away from that model, we are moving toward an era when it's more and more about personal branding.

Yes, you are a brand—and brand "*you*" is the only brand you should care about. Rather than devoting your time to elevating someone else's brand, you need to focus on cultivating one of your own.

What I love about personal branding is the human element, as well as the spirit of positivity. Unlike corporate brands that succeed by creating products that people like, personal brands are much more intimate.

The fact of the matter is that if you're in it for yourself and you are not providing anything of value, your personal brand will not succeed. Authenticity is at the heart of any successful personal brand. If you're offering a service, experience, or product that makes something better for someone else, your personal brand is going to do well.

This concept may still be foreign to some of you out there who are scratching your heads wondering, how am *I* a brand?

Simply put, in the age of the internet, resumes are dead. Google yourself—this is what an employer will do, in fact, this is what a prospective date or anyone who is curious about you will do. So, it is essential that you are in control of your reputation in real life *and* online.

---

[37] https://fortune.com/2016/05/10/baby-boomers-millennials-jobs/
[38] https://www.bls.gov/news.release/tenure.nr0.htm

Let's take a closer look at what goes into personal branding, and how you can be successful honing your own brand.

Big-Picture Thinking

We need to recognize that the world is changing much faster than we can see and much faster than we can even make sense of. I sat down with Stephan Spencer, a pioneering expert in SEO who came on the scene in the mid-'90s when most people had absolutely no concept of internet technology. Stephan is the author of multiple best-selling books, including The *Art of SEO* and *Google Power Search*. He elaborated on this concept of big-picture thinking.

Our brains are wired to understand a linear world. We see the horizon and think that it is the end of something, but we must remind ourselves that there is so much more than we can see. The horizon does not exist! It's a construct.

I asked Stephan how this is relatable to the career landscape and the business world. He spoke about the AI disruption happening in almost every industry.

What is the world going to be like in 2029—have you ever thought about this? Pick up a copy of Peter Diamandis' The Future is Faster Than You Think. *It is eye-opening stuff that we all need to be aware of. It may sound like something straight out of a Ridley Scott science-fiction movie, but the future really is faster than you think! AI will be writing blogs, scripts, whitepapers, emails, and on and on.*

Gone are the days of climbing the corporate ladder. As *Fortune* magazine editor Pattie Sellers famously said, careers are a jungle gym, not a ladder. Stephan added to this point:

Charles Darwin is often misquoted as having talked about "survival of the fittest," but what he actually stated in regard to which species climb the evolutionary ladder efficiently and effectively, is, "survival of the most adaptable."

If there is a possibility that AI will disrupt your area of expertise, how can you change your offering? What new niche will you create that is impermeable to this kind of inevitability? When I asked Stephan about pivoting, he said,

If you can bring two disparate disciplines together and you see the synergies, it's very hard for an AI to replace you.

Create Your Own Digital Space

Have a dedicated personal website. Stephan drove this point very succinctly when he emphasized:

You do not want to build your house on rented land!

I realized, in discussing this subject that I had long ago registered a domain in my name, but never followed through on creating my website. After interviewing Stephan, I dusted the cobwebs off my own website and even registered for Stephan's courses to continue to learn and do this properly from the start.

On the "About" page of your website, stand out by telling a story. Do this with a timeline. Check out Stephan's site, Stephanspencer.com as a great example. People engage with a story. How you struggled, overcame obstacles, persevered, learned new skills, reached goals. It humanizes you and builds on your personal brand as a thought leader.

Also, remember that if you're shy and have a need to remain private, you may lose a position you are trying to land to someone who has put him or herself out there. That is simply the way things work. Shrinking wallflowers do not land plum positions.

Results Leader

Rather than simply aiming to be a thought leader, you should be aiming to be a *results* leader. There is a way to toot your own horn by emphasizing the results you have been able to achieve. I am not talking about name-dropping and bragging, rather, telling stories of what you have accomplished. Do this with testimonials and case studies. And make sure they include the specifics and speak to any objections that your client may have had before hiring you. I asked Stephan about ways he has accomplished this on his site.

If your price at first seemed prohibitive and they almost chose not to hire you, tell what happened when they committed to hiring you. Did you deliver 10x or 100x what you cost them? Highlight these results. With this kind of specificity as to a client's return on investment, you will up your cache´ and increase your odds of being hired.

Search Engine Optimization

As I mentioned above, when someone applies for a job, the first thing any recruiter does is to search on the web and look at your digital footprint. Stephan emphasized that you must curate the first page of Google search for your name by controlling the narrative. Tell your story—don't let someone else tell it for you.

Do you have a knowledge panel on Google? Many are not aware of what a knowledge panel is. This is the rectangular panel that appears on the right side of the search results when you search for people, places, brands, events, etc. Google collects this data from public sources, including publications and Wikipedia, along with millions of objects and billions of relational facts. If you do not have a knowledge panel it is well worth the effort of attaining one because it is a designation of achievement and status, which is a huge plus.

LinkedIn is good for networking, but make sure you optimize your profile. Claim your custom linkedin.com URL. If your LinkedIn URL has a long number at the end of it, you didn't do this yet. Here's how to do that.[39] (see footnote for link)

Also, rather than reading like a resume, your LinkedIn profile should read like a sales letter.

You probably already have a Facebook profile, but do you have a Facebook page? If not, create one and list it under the category of "public figure."

Create Content

Depending on the industry you are in, you might want to have relevant tangential content for people who come to your website. Meaning, if you are a travel agent, write about an interesting new restaurant opening in a city your potential clients might like to travel to. Blogging is a great way to make your site attractive and relevant. Any accomplishment, accolade, published work, milestone—these all belong on your blog. Interact on social media through your content, which links back to your blog.

---

39   https://www.linkedin.com/help/linkedin/topics/6042/6054/87

Run Ads

All of us, myself included, have made the mistake of creating amazing content and then shouting in an empty room. You may have run ads for your clients, but how about running ads for yourself? Stephan suggests taking a great blog post that you created and running a Facebook ad for yourself. Upload an email list of your ideal employers to Facebook as a custom audience and target your ad to that list. A few dollars a day targeting those exact people you want to get in front of could pay off in spades.

Podcasts

Yes, there are a lot of podcasts out there already, but this is definitely still an avenue worth exploring. I asked Stephan how podcasting is a unique way of building your brand.

Podcasting is an intimate experience. It's an opportunity for you to speak into someone's ears while they're driving or walking or doing whatever activity. This is an incredibly powerful way to make an impression. You can choose topics on which you have become an expert, and you can also invite influential guests as guest speakers.

In regard to outside podcasts, pitch to be a guest on shows in your niche. Create a one-sheet and email it to podcasters with a well-crafted personalized email.

* * * *

In sum: look at the big picture, consider the task of building up your brand as a part-time job that will pay massive dividends. Position yourself as someone who understands the future, someone who is (and will continue to remain) relevant, and don't be afraid to proudly highlight your achievements. Remember, part of being successful is believing in yourself and convincing others how you will add value and drive results for them.

Build Your Personal Brand

1. Check your digital footprint. Are there things you would like to put forward that are not showing up? Are there things you don't want that *are* showing up? Remember page one of Google is all people will look at.

2. Chart a 30/60/90-day action plan to hone and build your personal brand. What are your objectives? If you are reading books and listening to podcasts for inspiration, building a website, creating a podcast, or developing content, be specific and realistic about a timeline for these kinds of goals. If you plan to blog, start a spreadsheet of possible topics, and create dynamic headlines. Remember, your brand takes some thought, and executing it will not be an overnight process.

3. Engage in social media platforms and link any blogs or articles back to your site.

BODY, MIND AND SOUL WELLNESS

"When we pay more attention to what keeps our energy up, what fascinates us, and what motivates us to wake up every day, we begin to connect the dots."

~ Dr. Toni Galardi

ONE OF THE advantages of being at a career crossroads is having the opportunity to assess whether you feel good physically, mentally, and spiritually, and if the career path you were pursuing was making that impossible, you get to determine how you can shift things to make your health a priority.

Showing you a simple process to keep your three-legged stool in harmony is the purpose of this book and it all starts with one simple word— awareness.

Whenever I see my guru, Sri Sri Ravishankar, he poses the same question to all of us: *Are you happy?* It may sound simplistic, but this one question summarizes everything so deeply and beautifully. In this section, I aim to help you figure out the answer for yourself.

I understand that there are days when it is impossible to be on schedule to eat right, exercise, sleep, meditate and laugh (yes, this should be on your schedule too!) but living a high-stress lifestyle for a long period of time can have a detrimental effect on your health. If the wellness leg of your three-legged stool is compromised, you may sit on the stool and not notice that anything is wrong. But every time you sit down the stool is getting weaker and you may be completely oblivious to the fact that it could break at any time. The stool might last for several more years or it may fall apart next month. Once this falls apart, you cannot enjoy the other two legs of your stool—friends/family and career, since both of them will require you to be mentally and physically healthy and happy.

To bring a body-mind-soul awareness, you must be intentional about forming habits that will bring this harmony in your life. It will not happen by accident, and it's not going to fall in your lap when you're sitting in the office putting in a twelve-hour day. When people refer to the mind-body-soul connection, the concept is that wellness is not just about physical health, it's a combination of having your physical and spiritual needs met. True wellness means you are not only taking care of yourself in a way that makes you feel healthy, inside and out, but you also feel a connection to nature and to the world around you. That awareness comes with first loving yourself because without self-love you won't be able to prioritize yourself or listen to what your body, mind, and soul are trying to tell you. To practice self-love, start by being kind, patient, and compassionate to yourself, the way you would be with someone else that you care about.

Body Wellness

The latest science suggests that maintaining physical fitness boosts our immune systems. So many common diseases, including heart disease, diabetes, and cancer are preventable by exercising and eating a healthy diet. If you're in good health you will also have an easier time combatting common viruses. According to the *New York Times*, "A series of 2005 experiments with mice, for instance, showed that if rodents jogged gently for about thirty minutes a day for several weeks, they were much more likely to survive a virulent form of rodent influenza than untrained animals."[40]

So many of us fall into unhealthy patterns when we work full-time, simply because we are not aware of what we're doing wrong, and we can't seem to find the time for ourselves over the course of a hectic day. I spoke with wellness coach Lisa Goldenthal, best-selling author of *The Boss Weight Loss*, who is a concierge-level wellness coach in Los Angeles. Lisa had a quote I love: "Sitting is the new smoking!" I asked her why sitting is so bad, and she pointed out:

So many activities we do involve sitting, whether we're at a desk, in a meeting, commuting, eating lunch, even chilling out on the couch during our downtime. We need to counteract all that inactivity with exercise.

Lisa works with her clients on specific exercises that counteract prolonged sitting. She also suggests getting a treadmill with a standing desk.

---

[40] https://www.ncbi.nlm.nih.gov/pubmed/15922557

The two essential habits Lisa stresses are establishing an exercise routine, and eating a healthy, sensible diet.

Lisa points out that it is not just what you eat, but *when* you eat that matters. For health, longevity, and weight loss, she highly recommends intermittent fasting. For her clients she recommends the 16/8 method. The concept is that you choose an eight-hour window of time to eat, for example 11:00 a.m. to 7:00 p.m. This way your body gets used to having fewer calories, and you actually boost your energy levels.

In terms of what to eat, Lisa stressed that, "It's not about diet, it's about lifestyle. We all know diets don't work long term." She suggests eating low-carb veggies like broccoli, cauliflower, spinach and salad, and high-quality protein (animal or plant) at every meal. Lisa also says you need to include healthy fats like wild-caught salmon, nuts, avocado, and coconut or olive oil.

Remember when I bought a HydroMATE motivation bottle after seeing Ashley Connell drinking from one? Lisa approves! She was emphatic on the importance of hydration. She advises calculating half of your body weight, converting that to ounces instead of pounds, and then drinking that amount in ounces of water to help keep you full and energized.

Mind Wellness

Mind wellness is directly related to our emotional well-being and the stress level in our life. Oftentimes we get stressed because we have too much to do and too little time/too few resources to do it. There are any number of other personal and professional situations that can cause you stress, and whether you're aware or not, your body tenses up over the course of the day whenever your mind is filled with too many "what ifs" and "if onlys."

The first exercise I would suggest for mind wellness is to go back to the exercise of turning FOMO to JOMO. Once you have the A-list of things that are essential in your life (mortgage, rent, bills, etc.) remember that those are the basics. If you're at the office all day long and you're feeling stressed out, try to find the balance by evaluating what areas are being neglected. The key is to first find contentment and joy in what you think you can do at a pace you can handle. Do not get caught up with where you are supposed to be in your career or compare yourself to someone else. There will always be someone doing bigger, better, and more fun things than you. This comparison with others is what brings more stress than we realize, and that additional stress further reduces our productivity, hampering our ability to achieve the things that we are capable of achieving.

Don't Bottle up Emotions

Find a way to rid yourself of any emotional baggage you are carrying around. Whether it's talking with friends, a therapist, or a life coach, there are so many support resources you can take advantage of both in-person and online. One of the benefits of taking time to share, process, emote, and being open to getting help is that eventually you let go of the stuff that may be holding you back. Get in touch with your feelings so that you can gain some understanding of what you are going through. Journaling was a powerful tool for me. When you write things down, you are processing the experiences in a way that is more concrete than just ruminating on things. If you are going through a rough phase in life, having trouble at work, about to yell at someone—write it down and feel the emotions as you write. You may find it is more productive to gather information about how you're feeling and to process your emotions than it is to lash out at someone else.

Meditation and Spiritual Knowledge

When people wake up in the morning, they begin to think about their problems—those problems are circuits, memories in the brain. Each one of those memories is connected to people and things at certain times and places, so the moment people start their day they're already thinking in the past. In an inspiring talk, memorialized on YouTube, Joe Dispenza explains how 95% of who we are by the time we're thirty-five is a memorized set of behaviors, emotional reactions, unconscious habits, hardwired attitudes, and perceptions that function like a computer program.[41] When you want to change, you're fighting this hardwiring. The hardwiring is difficult to reverse, but a meditation practice can actually change your brainwaves, slow them down, and when it's done properly, you are then able to make some really important changes in your life. In my own life, I can say that the spiritual practice I have maintained is the reason I'm alive and able to achieve what I set out to do these last few decades.

Soul Wellness

I recently got sucked into a very cute Pixar movie called *Soul*, where the main character has a bad accident and ends up in a purgatory of sorts called the Great Before. The purpose of the Great Before is to mentor fresh souls so that they can discover a "spark" that will drive them to a happy and productive life down on earth.

Of course, as I sat here writing this chapter the whole movie brought a big smile. It affirmed my belief that we need to reflect on our soul wellness daily, and not just after some major life incident makes you look back and wonder if maybe you put all your eggs in the wrong basket.

---

[41] https://www.youtube.com/watch?v=EpOMk1jOzgk&feature=share

What feeds and nourishes the soul can be different for different people and once again, don't get caught up in what works for others. One thing I have observed is that people overthink the issue of how to achieve soul wellness. There are no rules! It is not necessarily about doing charity work or devoting time to a cause and/or donating money. Let's not worry about redemption at this juncture, because the soul wellness I am referring to just means that you need to feed your soul.

I spoke to Jennifer McClure, CEO of Unbridled Talent & DisruptHR about ways to have an impact and feel good about it, no matter how grand or small-scale it is.

We tend to think that to have an impact, I need to start a nonprofit or, you know, feed the homeless or something that. While those things are certainly meaningful, if we paid attention to daily life, the people that often have the most impact on us are the people who took the time to send a text message just to say, 'thinking about you,' or someone who helped us carry something up the stairs.

We have all heard the expression, "that was a soul-sucking experience." So much of what we do can become stressful if we don't remember to feed our soul every day. Try to build a practice of enjoying your life because every day is a gift. Make a conscious effort to enjoy the simple pleasures. If you are eating a meal, enjoy every bite, and savor the flavors. If you are cooking, reading a book, programming, studying for exams, taking exams, going for a walk, doing your job that pays your bills, try to take deep breaths to relax and enjoy yourself. You will see a huge difference in productivity and happiness by just slowing down and breathing consciously throughout the day. I call this technique being in a continuous meditative state, which is commonly known as being present.

An important part of being present is sitting with your emotions before you react. This is all the more important when we are having tough times in relationships, whether at home or at work. If you can step back and take three deep breaths before you open your mouth to speak, or touch the keyboard to send an email, you will find there is a huge difference in the language you use, a difference so meaningful it will likely salvage many strained relationships.

Some other tips and suggestions to feed your soul are:

- Take some time to help others. Talk to your company to see if they have any service projects, if not, start one and do it with your office colleagues. Stepping outside of your situation and into someone else's can give you some perspective on life, and help you focus on someone other than yourself, which feels great.

- There is always someone who can see you as their role model who you can offer to mentor/advise and give a few minutes of your time. It is an incredibly gratifying experience.

- Invest in your hobbies or things that you love to do outside of work. Take music lessons, sports, cook, or any other creative activities that can give you a break. The key is to make it a part of your regular routine and not wait to go on vacation to enjoy doing these things once a year.

- Connect with nature and the environment around you. Do some gardening even if it is in pots in your apartment. Walk, hike, play with kids, or run with your dog. When you take a walk in nature, pay attention to your senses. What are three things you can touch, three things you can smell, three things you can see, three things you can taste, and three things you can hear? Connecting with nature is good for the body, mind, and soul.

Whatever your happy place is, whatever rituals you can establish to lighten your load and feed your soul, it's critical that you make them a priority. If you do, you will find you are more in tune with nature, more engaged in the world, and that you have an undeniable sense of fulfillment and meaning in your life.

Unconscious Laughter

It's sad to say that while an average four-year-old laughs three hundred times a day, adults laugh only fifteen times a day. I'm not sure how accurate these numbers are, but it's obvious that children laugh way more than adults. We have lost this amazing skill in the race to grow up and achieve things and I believe that we are heading into a serious laughter crisis. In fact, there is a term, gelotology, which means the study of laughter. According to Psychology Today, "Research done by Ramon Mora-Ripoll, medical scientific director at Organizacién Mundial de la Risa, Barcelona Spain, has shown that humor and laughter is related to health, and can release physical and emotional tension, improve immune functioning, stimulate circulation, elevate mood, enhance cognitive functioning and, not surprisingly, increase friendliness."[42]

You may think you need to go out to see rom coms, read funny columns, or watch your favorite comedian's videos to laugh out loud, but a laughing practice can actually be cultivated. I recently learned an important lesson from Dr. Madan Kataria, founder of Laughter Yoga.

"Laughter should be unconditional. Natural laughter that courses through our life depends upon many reasons and conditions, but the fact is that there are not many reasons which make us laugh. In laughter yoga, we do not leave laughter to chance, rather, we do it out of

---

42 https://www.psychologytoday.com/us/blog/talking-about-trauma/201311/lol-how-laughter-can-improve-your-health

commitment. This is a guaranteed way of getting the health benefits of laughter. Scientific studies have shown that our body can not differentiate between spontaneous laughter and intentional laughter. We will get the same benefits either way."

He started this program twenty-five years ago with just five people in a park in Mumbai. At this point, Dr. Kataria can proudly say that they have helped millions of people in over 100+ countries change their lives simply by following his amazing laughter techniques. There are laughter clubs all over the world where strangers just come and laugh together without any reason. I must say, though I have utilized several wellness practices over the years, I always felt something was missing. When I discovered laughter yoga, it felt like the missing piece of the puzzle. What really intrigued me is that practicing laughter is just like any other exercise, I even discovered a laughter yoga dance online, which I am thoroughly enjoying.

It's time to get serious about laughter. It will make you live happier and longer!

Your BMS Rating / Happiness Scale

We discussed several ways to address overall wellness. I have been referred to as a data and process freak, so of course, I had to come up with a simple way to chart and analyze this and create a process for it.

Being fit will be easy when you have the right process in place. The first step is to start writing down your physical fitness habits, including how you are moving, exercising, and eating. Analyze if you are on the right track and find areas for improvement and then create a sustainable and realistic plan that you can follow without stressing out.

Quantifiable body-mind-soul wellness is something I like to call a BMS rating. It's something you can measure for yourself because only you will know when you are out of alignment. Every day around the same time, you should rate yourself in each category, body-wellness, mind-wellness, soul-wellness, from 1–10. Don't be hard on yourself if you do poorly one day. The key is transparency and awareness.

Now take the average of all three categories, with the top score being thirty and the bottom score being three. If the number you come up with feels low to you, think about what score you would realistically like to attain. Set that as a goal to reach within a certain time period. Once again there is no right or wrong answer as it is a relative score for you and the only person you are competing with is your past self. It's as simple as that. Someday, you may feel really happy and satisfied at a 10% score and some days you may score 80% and feel like you can do better. Yes, it's possible that it can happen.

Some years ago, I was driving and one of the front tires of my car suddenly flew off. I had to manage to drive on three wheels to park before calling for help. Fortunately, I did not have even a scratch and I survived—that day my score was off the charts as I was just feeling happy to be alive, and that was the only thing that mattered.

Now let's bring this BMS rating to your happiness scale. Think about all the things on your list you created in Section One that give you happiness—relationships, finances, health, travel, and career. Try not to have more than ten things both materialistic and non-materialistic. Once again rate on the scale of 1–10 where you stand on achieving those and create an average to get your daily (or weekly, or monthly) happiness scale.

I had a chance to get some wisdom on this topic from Khurshed Batliwala, program director at the Art of Living and author of several books including *Happiness Express*. Every time I see him he's always smiling, radiant, and full of energy. It was quite encouraging to hear him talk about rating in a similar, simple way.

"It's just that people can list out significant areas of their life, whatever is important for them and rate themselves from a scale of zero to ten and then take a percentage, if they are above 70%, then they are reasonably happy.

Now the real question is not what their scale shows but what do they want it to be and what they are going to do about it? If they are satisfied with a score of 60% then it's ok, but if they want it to be 80% then how are they going to get there?"

* * * *

So, we learned the importance of loving ourselves and listening to our body, mind, and soul. We learned to raise our awareness and simply to take care of ourselves. If we are not happy then it will be impossible to make others around us happy. Let's focus on being the source of happiness, so we can help spread it around.

Let's Start Loving Ourselves

1. The first step is to explore and know yourself by journaling your schedule, mood, diet, exercise, emotional experience, social interactions, gratitude, or work hours. Journal everything you do from the time you wake up to the time you go to sleep. If you journal for two to three weeks, you'll find it's much easier to measure and track.
2. Once you know yourself, start looking for areas where you think you can do better. In regard to your physical well-being, can you take a few minutes to stretch between long work hours, or take

a walk while you are talking to someone on the phone? Can you eat with awareness and enjoy your meal instead of rushing through it; can you take a few deep breaths and smile while talking to people? Try to carve out some simple ways to improve yourself, to be more effective and efficient. You will notice that the same task will start to give you a bit more joy every time you do it with awareness. That's the secret sauce. That's the path that leads to happiness.

3. On a daily or weekly basis, track your BMS rating and happiness score. Continue to see how it can improve and don't be discouraged if it goes down. The key is to be aware that it is going down, and that you and only you can make it go up and the way you do that is by creating a plan that will get you there.

FAMILY, FRIENDS AND YOUR SUPPORT SYSTEM

"Let us be grateful to the people who make us happy; they are the charming gardeners who make our souls blossom."

~ Marcel Proust

LIFE CAN BE challenging. If you are wise, no matter how busy your life gets, always check in with your family and friends. Cultivate those friendships and keep those connections strong because when the going gets tough, if you have the love and support of those special people in your inner circle, you can handle anything. Whether it's an unexpected kindness, a big thing or a little thing, or just someone who knows you who listens and cares, these are the kind of soul wellness components that will sustain you in good times, and in hard times too.

Interestingly, because many people suddenly began working remotely in 2020, the pandemic was an eye-opening experiment for one partner to get a taste of what the other partner deals with on a daily basis. When talking about this issue with Scott Jorgensen, senior executive at Salesforce as well as an advisor to Mom Relaunch, he wished there were a guide for family members to learn how to participate and take care of the things that were never on their to-do lists before. This chapter is that much-needed guide.

If you are a busy, working, single parent going it on your own, these kinds of issues need to be worked out, and they are best worked out by creating a support system—whether it's a parent, grandparent, friend, or neighbor, who can pitch in and help.

Communication

I am always surprised when I hear how many men and women assume roles in their partnership that they don't actually want. When people drift into roles unintentionally, it builds resentment. This is another reason to always check in with that vision of your three-legged stool. If your life is becoming unbalanced and you are unhappy, communicate this to your partner. Friction on the home front only gets more pronounced when it isn't acknowledged or dealt with. Scott spoke about his new normal, working from home during the COVID-19 lockdown, and pointed out that while before, he and his wife were having separate experiences—he was at the office during the day, and she was at home—there actually is an opportunity now to share in each other's experience while setting some boundaries around work and family integration under one roof.

Everybody's daily routine was disrupted, and I was in denial about how stressful this was. I am highly influenced by my environment. When working from home, I'd go out to the kitchen for a break and there was so much going on that my brain was chaotic. I'd go back into my office and I'd feel overwhelmed. My wife and kids and I decided to have a plan. How are we going to have an awesome life together during this lockdown? So, we came up with the Jorgensen Awesome Family Plan. For example, one massive action plan is listed as: Time with friends (exercise, creative, Roblox/cooperative game). Then, the result: Have a great time. The purpose: Make lockdown seem/feel better. These are the four categories he would stress as a guide to creating a good support system.

- *Be aware you have an opportunity to be more a part of things. Be aware of what is going on with your family. I like to keep a journal because it gives me clarity, and it feels more tangible when I write things down.*
- *Be aware of what's going on with friends and social connections.*
- *Be aware of what's going on with work.*
- *Find the unique opportunities. For example, I can look at the kid's schedules, take a break, and go down the hall to see how my daughter is feeling after her math test. Usually, she is at school and I'm at work, so this is a rare chance for us to connect in the middle of a school day.*

Emotional Help

We spoke to Curtis Blodgett, owner of Beach Bee Meadery in New Jersey. Curtis worked for Hitachi for many years selling data storage plans, a job that required international travel, business dinners several times a week, and long hours at the office. Originally, his wife Madeleine was a stay-at-home parent, until she segued into earning a master's degree and began a teaching career. Curtis had some thoughtful input on the subject of emotional support.

The first thing that comes to mind is patience. My mind may have been focused on twenty different things, but, when I walked in the door, I really tried to be present in the moment with Madeleine and spend time focusing on what is important to her. Even though you're off in the world making deals and you may be attaining some level of success, letting your ego get in the way at home is a big problem—it's just going to create a lot of division. If you find you can let your ego take a backseat to the responsibility that you feel, you're going to feel more connected with your family.

I asked him how he manages to prevent outside forces from affecting the relationship, and he stressed the importance of hearing each other out and compromising.

Compromise is a skill you need to learn in marriage. No one is king, and no one is queen. You can argue your point and insist that you're right and get really mad, but at the end of the day, anger is a super-wasted emotion. With Madeleine I will say, OK, I get to win the next fight! I'm more about compromise than confrontation. I don't hold onto things and I always made it a point after Madeleine and I got in an argument to say to the kids, 'Oh, I've got to go and apologize to Mom.' And they saw that. It made an impression on them.

And the best nuggets we got from Curtis—something he and Madeleine heard once on the *Tonight Show with Johnny Carson* that stuck with them:

Always end the day with a kiss!

Make Their Day

The work of running a household can be challenging, and at times overwhelming. We all get mired in mundane routines that can feel uninspiring. I am a firm believer that along with making time for each other to reconnect and check in at the end of the day, it is also incredibly important to sprinkle in some element of surprise. This is a secret weapon—something you can pull out of your back pocket to change things up, even if it is just something that was on their to-do list that you are handling on the sly.

A well-thought-out surprise is so much more impactful than flowers or chocolate. The message is, *I see all that you do, and I want to take one thing off your plate to make your day a little easier.* You might get creative and gas up the car or take a dreaded chore off their list and slyly do it while they are at work. Imagine the genuine smile on your partner's face when they are getting up, ready to do some of their mundane chores only to realize that you have already done it for them. From my personal experience, this brings a lot of joy. It does not happen very often in my home, but when it happens it feels great.

Use Each Other's Strengths and Do Not Dwell on the Weaknesses

My friend Vinita Gupta, (no relation, though we share the same last name) had wise words to say about the support system at home as it relates to couples who both work and are raising children together. Vinita is a highly successful entrepreneur and was the first Indian American woman to take her company public in the U.S.

I was an idealist. I thought it should be a 50-50 partnership. Little did I know, it's never 50-50. That is really just a fantasy! You ask a man, and he thinks he's getting the short end of the 50-50, and you talk to the woman and she thinks she is getting the short end.

Instead of striving for that elusive 50-50 workload, look for how you can have one partner handle things they are good at. My mother used to say, "Don't expect fish to fly."

In my house, while I end up responsible for household chores, my partner handles the finances and investments. It may sound stereotypical, but after so many attempts at trying to understand the finances and investments, I just can't get there. These things come naturally to my husband, and he is happy to handle them.

Task List

With the Jorgensens as inspiration, get to the basics of creating a task list and distribute household responsibilities. They managed to make this a fun family activity and Scott noted that the kids were more invested in following through on tasks since they were partners in creating the document.

Set expectations as early as possible to avoid conflicts. Attach a result and a purpose to each task. The key to not letting small resentments spiral into larger issues is to increase the awareness of imbalance and mounting frustration; recognize that it's happening and break free of it.

Hangout with Friends

According to a Harvard Health study, social connections "not only give us pleasure, but they also influence our long-term health in ways every bit as powerful as adequate sleep, a good diet, and not smoking. Dozens of studies have shown that people who have satisfying relationships with family, friends, and their community are happier, have fewer health problems, and live longer."[43]

On average, people have three to five close friends in their inner circle. Those of you who worry that you need to run out and make new friends because you only have a few close friends can relax. Friends come into our lives at different stages, and they fill different needs. When we're young we are generally much more open to making new friends, but as we get older work and life can get in the way of devoting time to friendships. Be aware if you're neglecting this leg of your stool, and work on balancing it out.

Everyone has their own way of connecting and bonding with people, so this is not another writeup about how to find friends. It's more important to focus on the quality of your friendships rather than the quantity. You should generally feel joyful about your relationships with friends. While we're all leading such busy lives, time spent with friends should fill you up and add a positive dimension to your day. If you get this joy by just hanging out with neighbors, your friends online, in the park, or at the gym it should give you the sense that you both are enjoying your get-togethers so much that time is flying.

Remember to always be open to letting new people into your life. Look for opportunities to connect whenever and wherever you can to talk to people. You never know when that special friend will walk into your life. If you feel reserved about starting conversations with strangers, then apply some of the networking techniques we discussed earlier. These will work in your personal life too.

Above all, stay positive. You may find if you smile and say hello and have a friendly air about you then it's easier for you to connect with people. After getting my dog, Rocky, I spoke to so many neighbors I didn't know—strangers in the dog park, and even people

---

[43] https://www.health.harvard.edu/newsletters/harvard_womens_health_watch/2010/december

who gave me puppy-training tips. I enjoyed every moment of those interactions even though I may never see these people again. Simply getting out of your house, out of your office, and out in the world interacting with another human being makes you feel part of something, and definitely helps feed the soul.

Importance of Extended Family

One of the stark differences I find in social interaction today is the shift of mindset from "we" to "me." In past generations, it was much more common to live close by or in the same household with our extended family members, however today, extended families may only get together on rare occasions, like weddings and funerals. Travel behavior has shifted away from planning trips to meet extended family and shifted more toward fancy trips alone, with friends, or with your immediate family. I'm not discouraging vacations, as I myself am an avid traveler. I'm simply pointing out that as we become more individualistic and less connected to our own relatives, we lose something as a society. So many movies and TV-shows depict relatives as irksome and a general nuisance, and that sentiment has permeated how we look at extended families.

Try to make a genuine effort at having a relationship with your maternal and fraternal relatives. Having a shared family background can be a bonding experience, despite the generational differences that exist. Sharing genealogy with people connects you to your past, and if you maintain relationships with relatives it can really add a layer of rich connection to your life.

Remember, it's never too late to reconnect. Investing time in building and maintaining positive and healthy relationships with your extended family broadens your support system and will bring your BMS rating way up.

* * * *

Whether or not you're in a committed relationship, whatever kind of support system you are part of is only as strong as each and every person involved. How can we cheer each other on and more properly communicate what we need from our loved ones in order to remain in balance? Think of ways in which you need support, and ways in which you can extend emotional and practical support in return.

Let's Improve Our Social Connections Skills

1. When observing your household, what habits seem most important to everyone? How are family members choosing to meet their core needs: certainty, variety, significance, connection, growth, contribution? Where might you adjust to complement each other?

2. If your stool feels imbalanced because work got in the way of friendships, make a list of acquaintances you'd like to get to know better, and old friends you'd like to reconnect with. Reach out to everyone on your list and start prioritizing reconnecting with old friends and making new ones.

3. If you miss your extended family, take the incentive to organize an informal reunion. It can be a picnic or restaurant date, or simply a backyard hangout. Don't wait for the next wedding or funeral to happen.

CHECKLIST

Please continue to use the workbook you downloaded earlier.

Before you proceed to the next section, make sure you have the following things in place:

1. Knowing that many fields have (or will in the near future) experience disruption, how do you plan to keep your curiosity and knowledge growing?

2. Have you created your own personal advisory board—people who genuinely care about your success?

3. Three immediate things you will do to flex your networking muscle.

4. Have you practiced your elevator pitch?
5. What is your wellness routine? How do you practice self-care every day?
6. How many close friends do you have where both of you feel the joy of togetherness?
7. Are you getting the support you need from your partner/family? If not, how can they better support your career ambition?

PART THREE

RELAUNCH
HOW TO BE WHAT YOU WANT TO BE

The first two sections in the book were all about taking a deep dive. We wanted to assess where you are and look at everything involved in creating the work-life harmony that will balance your three-legged stool. You learned tools and strategies that prepare you to not only achieve professional success, connect with the people and the world around you, as well as mind, body, and soul wellness.

In the third section, we're going to move forward with an individualized plan. You're going to be deciding what you want your life to be, you're going to be choosing the career path that feels right, and then you're going to map out a plan that allows you to boldly and confidently take those necessary next steps. Don't expect overnight results, but you need to start moving in the right direction, as well as consciously make choices that align with your talents and your vision. It's time to play to your strengths and connect all the dots.

CHOOSE YOUR PATH TO SUCCESS

"Your life is a collection of choices. Every day is a new chance to make a new choice, a better choice."

~ **David Heinemeier Hansson**

AT THIS POINT, you have done all the exercises designed to help you understand who you are, what your secret sauce is, and what makes you happy. Now it's time to choose the right career path to help you achieve your goals.

New possibilities are exciting but choosing can feel overwhelming because there are so many factors to take into consideration. The purpose of this chapter is to take a three-dimensional look at the different paths—what you can expect from that path, what your day will be like, and the realities (and myths) of each.

In order for you to know which path to take, you have to be able to see the options in a way that paints a picture so clear you can see yourself in that role. And while there are multiple ways to achieve your goals, we are going to focus here on three distinct paths. Please note that you can pick and choose what works for you from the different paths and create your own journey if that suits you better. The three paths we will focus on are:

- Entrepreneurship
- Traditional career/job
- Freelance, aka one-person army

There are so many misconceptions out there, it makes it hard to have an accurate three-dimensional picture of what each path will look like. And that's why it is so important to start with deconstructing the myths of these paths first. After that, we can learn about each path in an immersive way so that you can make a proper choice.

Clearly, the theory behind doing a thing is quite different than actually placing yourself in that day-to-day experience. How can you possibly understand the pace, lifestyle, and pros and cons of working for yourself, starting a business, or going down a traditional career path? There is no generic answer to this. It's a very personal decision. It is for exactly this reason that we created workshops to provide people at a career crossroads with experiential hands-on learning. Through immersive, interactive exercises participants get a simulated experience that puts them inside that world and gives them a chance to experiment and learn. People get to learn about themselves, and about this potential career path. Anyone who participates in the workshop will emerge with a realistic idea of what this work looks like, what next steps they'll need to take, and can then go forward confidently with the tools they will need to achieve success in any profession.

Before you start on any path, you should be deeply committed to why you are doing this, and always refer back to that "why." It is also important to assess all the things that could go wrong (aka, not according to plan). This technique—negative visualization—is an exercise that lets you sit with the worst outcome and see how it makes you feel. Entrepreneur and author David Heinemeier Hansson is the person who brought the negative visualization idea to my attention. The idea sounds so negative but listening to David's advice was so refreshing and spot-on. Also listening to his Danish accent had a calming effect on me!

The concept of negative visualization is that if you are aware at the outset of all the different possible outcomes, you won't feel blindsided emotionally or financially if things don't go as planned. Be prepared for failures. I asked David to elaborate on this.

You can't let even the worst outcome drain you emotionally or financially.

To that I would add, you also cannot let it take your smile away. However hard the journey may be, if you think you can still walk out saying that this was a valuable experience and that you had an opportunity for personal and professional growth, then you are on the right path.

Entrepreneurial Path

Although David is a successful entrepreneur, he considers his advice to be the countermelody to the stereotypical entrepreneurial advice.

The musical analogy, which he attributes to Derek Sivers,[44] is this: underneath the main melody you have a countermelody that goes against the main melody and together they make harmony. This is David's way of saying that he would like to inspire others to see that there are multiple ways to approach starting up a venture of your own. And like the countermelody, your path can stand on its own, creating its own unique music.

Debunking Those Tired Myths about Entrepreneurship

- Entrepreneurs are guys in their late twenties in Silicon Valley

No! This is not a field exclusive to men. Anyone at any age can start up a venture of his or her own. In fact, seasoned, experienced entrepreneurs have several things on their side that the younger person does not—connections, knowledge of the industry, and the wisdom that comes with age and experience. And no, you do not have to be in Silicon Valley to be an entrepreneur, especially if yours is not a tech-related venture.

Diane Flynn, co-founder, and CEO of ReBoot Accel reinforces this point as well:

There are all these statistics saying that older entrepreneurs are much more likely to succeed. I think it's partly their connections—they're well connected. I also think it's largely because of pattern recognition. They've probably failed before—many times. And they're not going to do the same thing again.

- You have to have a built-in network

---

44   https://sive.rs/counter

No doubt having a strong network will help but not having one shouldn't be a deterrent. You will build the network as you run the business. To use my example, I ran my business remotely (and solo) from home, which was quite unusual for CEOs during those days. I came to terms with the fact that I wouldn't be in a culture of meeting for drinks or dinner after work. I even stayed home during lunch and mostly ate with my family. I stayed connected with people online but couldn't develop relationships by dining and team building and knowing them personally.

Now that things have been shaken up and much of the world is suddenly working remotely, people are realizing how difficult it is to network from afar. It's not easy, but if you reach out creatively, connections can be made, and relationships can deepen. You just need to put in the effort to make it happen.

- It's all or nothing

Another stereotype about becoming an entrepreneur is that you've got to sacrifice everything and devote eighty hours a week to making a go of it. I asked David what he thought about that, and he was quite entertaining:

Almost every single write-up is the same bullshit about how they had three credit cards and they maxed them out and then they took a third mortgage on their house and on and on, right? Because that makes for a good story. The truth is, starting a business on the side while keeping your day job can provide all the cash flow you need.

When David co-founded Basecamp, that is exactly what he did. They started small, did not take outside money, and they grew the business to the point where he could then commit to it as a full-time venture. Lesson learned: go at your own pace.

- The freedom of not having a boss

If you want to answer to no one then this will be one of the worst reasons to be an entrepreneur. When I sat down and spoke with Jen Sargent, CEO of Wondery, and founder of HitFix on this topic, she smiled and said, "This is one of the most misunderstood facts about entrepreneurship. If a customer gives you a new requirement on Friday that has to be completed first thing on Monday, you have no choice but to work all weekend."

Speaking from my experience running my own companies, I always feel that my clients and my employees are all my bosses in a way. You've got to make payroll and meet all your employee's needs, which is a big responsibility. If cash flow is tight one month, this will be stressful for you. And while you have no boss, it does not mean you have no one to answer to. One of the tradeoffs of being the boss is not being able to walk out the door and leave work behind at the office.

- If you build a product, customers will come

People often have the misconception that if you have a great idea, you can have a great company. This is not necessarily so. Starting out with a great idea is like a chef starting out with a counter full of fresh, raw ingredients. The amazing meal does not happen on its own—it happens because of timing, finesse, talent, and proper use of those quality ingredients. Similarly, making a business successful involves a great deal of planning, communication, vision, and effective execution. Behind the glamor of that great idea is a lot of blood, sweat, and tears!

- You have to go after investors

Around 77% of small businesses primarily fund themselves through personal savings and finance. Many multinational corporations were founded with $20,000 or less in savings. However, 82% of failed businesses go under due to cash-flow problems.

The biggest challenge that most business owners face is figuring out how much money they need to leverage a proportionate scaling plan.

Tim Draper, Venture Capital investor and author of the book *Startup Hero*, explains beautifully and simply why one might consider an entrepreneurial path.

Entrepreneurship is a calling. A true entrepreneur cannot keep themselves from becoming an entrepreneur. Entrepreneurship can be learned though. Before you leave your job to become an entrepreneur, ask yourself if you really want to dedicate your life to this purpose. Great entrepreneurs make a great sacrifice for the good of their customers.

If you head down this path, be aware that you may end up giving up a forty-hour workweek only to realize there are additional demands on your time. There may be more freedom in some areas, but on the flip side, there may be more obligations in places where you didn't have to bother while you were in a traditional career. When you're an employee, the responsibility of keeping the lights on and keeping a business afloat is not your problem. As an entrepreneur, that's a pretty weighty responsibility.

Traditional Job Path

Not everyone should be an entrepreneur. I have had excellent employees over the years who were great at their jobs and appreciated the opportunity to work in a traditional career with a salary and benefits.

Deconstructing the Myths about Being an Employee for a Company

- You're a sucker

A lot of the stereotypes put out there about entrepreneurs imply that people with "regular" jobs are suckers. David put this so well:

Almost every entrepreneurial propaganda story involves how people are essentially suckers, right? Because hey, you could build your own empire, you could be Elon Musk firing rockets into space and all these other things. So, you should feel bad if you don't have that level of ambition. And I think it's just as important to flip that around and say, you know what, the world is full of satisfied people who have a job.

- You have no freedom in a 9–5 job

This all depends on how you define freedom. If you're starting up a business you may not be able to take a vacation for years, and though it's true that if you are the boss you can set your own hours, many people with 9–5 jobs appreciate the freedom of leaving work behind at the end of the day. As an entrepreneur, it is more difficult to have that boundary. While structure can feel suffocating to some, to others it is a relief to know that when you're at work, you're "on," and when you leave, your evenings and weekends are your own.

- Steady income

Traditional career paths are not as safe as they once were. Because job security in the private sector is not what it once was, employees aren't always able to rely on that steady, reliable income. Author, Rick Wartzman, says that jobs offering security, decent wages, and good benefits are becoming harder to find, in part because of automation, globalization, and the weakening of unions. Anyone can be laid off. If you are reading this book it's very likely you have faced it personally. The purpose of many of the exercises we have taken you through in *Career Interrupted* is precisely so that should you get let go from one job, you will be able to pivot to another situation quickly.

- You're limiting your potential

This is obviously a broad generalization that cannot possibly be applied to having a job. At this point, you know all about being a lifelong learner and working to remain effective and relevant in your field, so there is no reason why your potential in any career should be limited.

In fact, many people are under the misconception that if you love doing what you do, you should start your own company. The truth is, whether you're a writer creating a content business, or a developer looking into starting up a company, you will be doing less and less writing and developing and more and more tasks which you may not be cut out for and may not even like.

The trick is to find a company that won't suck the life out of you, where you can shine and continue to master your expertise.

Becoming a One-Person Army

Some people have a distaste for the corporate world, and they prefer a freer format with no hierarchy and no set structure. And they're not alone. According to Staffing Industry Analysts (SIA), in 2019, there were fifty-four million contingent workers in the US, representing 34% of all workers, generating $1.3 trillion in revenue. By their definition, a contingent worker is anyone earning money by performing work that has a limited tenure from the client's perspective, whether a summer intern or an outside consultant brought in for a project.

I refer to this as being a one-person army because whether you signed up for this or not, you are running a business. Additionally, because you are your own CEO, accountant, salesperson, and project manager, there will be tasks you need to work on that are outside your talents. If you're not someone who can be happy dealing with the ups and downs of running a business, then this may not be the right career choice for you.

Debunking Freelancer Myths

- Flexible Schedule

Many companies are moving toward a remote-working model, so if you're thinking you'd have more flexibility freelancing, that all depends. Certainly, there is a lot to be said for setting your own hours and having only yourself to answer to, but deadlines are deadlines, and if you have multiple clients, you must stay on the ball and make sure you are managing your time well so that you can meet all their needs.

As I mentioned above, having less structure does allow more freedom, but you must then be responsible to prioritize your tasks and motivate yourself to find your productive self.

- Great lifestyle

Yes, you will go at your own pace and work at home, and at coffee shops, and co-working spaces. But it's important to note that working remotely for yourself can be an isolating lifestyle. No one speaks to each other at co-working spaces because you're all strangers. If your work style is very social and interactive, you may find you get lonely off on your own all day long.

- No limit to earning potential

There is definitely value in deciding your own pay rate but managing your deliverables and chasing work to make sure you have enough clients/jobs/projects can be exhausting. If you go through a dry spell, not only do you need to have resources saved up, but you'll also need to hit the pavement and start drumming up new business. Make sure when you opt for this freedom that you also realize you are responsible for your own health insurance payments, quarterly taxes, and retirement savings, which can be a substantial chunk of money to set aside from your freelancing income. If you haven't been disciplined during the year, filing your taxes can be a very stressful experience.

- Work on interesting projects only

You may indeed build up to a level where you can pick and choose the work you prefer to do, but realistically, there may be times when you take work to meet your expenses, even if it's not ideal work. If you're a freelance content creator there is no guarantee that the work you find will always be the work you prefer. If you are willing to put in the time and the footwork, remember that you've got to keep on hustling and be willing, at first, to take work simply because it pays the bills.

Some high-level points to keep in mind as you make your choice:

- Financial situation and security. This is one of the most important factors in determining your choice. Sometimes, we end up making decisions where financial pressure is the primary motivation, unable as we are at the time to allow our personal preference to dictate our course of action. If you find yourself in this situation then don't cause yourself further stress. Go with the flow of what makes logical sense at this time but work extra hard and manage your finances in a way that can help you make better choices next time.

- Risk tolerance. This is a very subjective topic, and everyone has different tolerance levels. The key is to identify what your risk levels are. Once again, go back to your alignment framework and see what your vision and values are, and make decisions accordingly. No matter what path you choose, give yourself enough cushion and go with the idea that your choice may not work. Have a backup strategy so that in case things don't work out as planned, you will be prepared.

- Work-life harmony. It's very easy to compare our situation with other people's lives but we forget that everyone has a unique story and most likely dealt with struggles of their own to get to where they are. Think about what work-life harmony looks like and feels like for you, within the two constraints listed above.

- Health insurance. Yes, this is (and should be) a massive deciding factor in anyone's thought process when it comes to deciding on a career path. Healthcare is exorbitant, and this is just an unfortunate fact of life living in this country. No matter what career choice you make, please ensure that you have great health coverage for yourself and your dependents.

* * * *

I do understand that making a big life decision like this can be extremely difficult and no matter how much we talk about the pros and cons of each path, only you can sit with the experience and make a proper decision.

There will be times when you want to give up, and that's when all the work you did to build your alignment framework will come in handy and keep you inspired to go on this journey. There will be times when you feel like you're not moving forward, but a quick look at the vision and values you set for yourself will assure you that you're on track. There will be times when you want to hand in your resignation and just focus on your business full-time. But you won't, because the math you did will tell you this isn't the right time. All that research and planning will help you stay on the path you choose to pursue. And every time you feel like maybe this path isn't for you, look and get inspired by the people who have walked on this path. They did it. You can do it too.

What Path Is Right for You?

1. What did you learn in debunking the myths of these different career paths? What specifically drew you to that path, or made you definitely think of *not* choosing that path?
2. Practice negative visualization on your selected path. Be aware of your emotions and reactions as you work on this exercise. Are these consequences you are willing to accept and work through?
3. State what your objective is, and the best path you feel you can take to help you achieve your goals. Discuss your plan with your mentors/advisors and with your loved ones so they all can help support you and guide you on your journey.

HOW TO PULL OFF A SUCCESSFUL CAREER CHANGE

"We keep moving forward, opening new doors and doing new things because we're curious, and curiosity keeps leading us down new paths."

~ **Walt Disney**

PIVOTAL CAREER CHANGES are becoming more and more common, especially for people coming back from a career break. Look beyond your skills and think of other interests, perhaps something that you may have put on the back burner for practical reasons. If you've done the introspection, created an alignment framework, and done the work honing your core competencies and you have made the bold decision to change careers, congratulations! You're ready to take action to transition to this next phase of your professional life.

Many of the steps in the previous chapter will apply here, and there are a few distinct strategies to apply when you are pivoting in a new career direction as well.

Work with a Career Doctor/Therapist/Coach

If you have the resources, this would be an excellent time to reach out to a good career coach. This is a growing field, though it may still be a foreign concept to some. While people generally do not hesitate to reach out for medical help when they have a physical problem, they often are reluctant to reach out for therapy or coaching when they need it the most. A career crossroads is one of those times.

I interviewed a motherhood clarity mentor in the *Parental Indecision* chapter, which is an example of a very specialized kind of coach. I also interviewed Ted Capshaw, who was an invaluable resource for Kim Sneeder when she was at a career crossroads. Career coaches help you achieve clarity around your professional goals. There is definitely an element of therapy involved because you are not just exploring your options, you are assessing where you are at in your professional trajectory and in your life and deciding on next steps. It's important to vet the coach you are going to work with and make sure he or she has experience in the field you are interested in. Luckily, no matter where you currently live, there are many excellent options online.

Try Things On

Depending on your financial situation, you can keep your steady job while you try new things. Start up a side hustle. The availability of technology platforms and the change in work culture has made this a much more conceivable avenue. If the side hustle takes off, then it makes sense to pivot with confidence.

Think of ways you can explore the career you are interested in without committing. Yes, you may think you are too old for an internship but shadowing someone or apprenticing can be a great way to get a feel for what their day looks like, and it will give you a concrete idea of everything the job actually entails. You might establish some important connections this way, as well.

Before committing to any specific job or role, try as many options as possible. Talk to as many people as you can who are in the career path you are exploring. Understand the pros and cons and see if this work aligns with your framework. Explore with an open mind and don't put any expectations on it.

Combine Disciplines

If you are someone who worked as a location scout on film productions and you want a steadier job, perhaps you could take your passion for finding locations and properties as well as your experience knowing your city inside-out and try to get hired by a real estate agency. Though your experience is not directly related, they may be impressed with what you have accomplished, and they may appreciate you would need less training than a recent college grad who does not understand the nuances of the region.

Another example is if you have a background in childcare or teaching and you want to pivot to an educational non-profit, there is a lot about your experience that would make you a desirable candidate, if you promote yourself and your credentials properly.

Confidence and positivity are really the keys to pivoting careers. Remember that companies value people who are agile and keen on learning new things. If you have impressive accomplishments on your resume, talk about them in your interview, and draw clear connections from your accomplishments and passions to all that you can contribute to this new position.

Reach Out to Your Wider Network

Your network is your best friend at this time. Reach out to as many people in the industry you are interested in and request them to talk to you, advise you, and hopefully refer you to jobs in their company.

When you reach out to your network

- Make sure you communicate a clear understanding of your ask from them. Be as precise as possible. Ideally, you can send a job link to them and then
    - Ask them for connections, referrals, advice, etc.
    - Frankly ask them if they think you would be a good fit for the position, if not then ask for suggestions of how you can better prepare yourself.
- Request introductions and share your information in their network.
- Find out if they are open to being your referral based on whatever experience you have knowing them or working with them both for soft skills and job-related skills.

Think Outside the Box

Thinking outside the box does not just pertain to making contacts and following up with them, it's also about leaning into your intuition. Think about your dream job. Are these possible or impossible dreams? If you feel you don't fit the racial/gender profile for this job, you should not let that stop you. I asked Gwendolyn Turner about diversity initiatives. She believes that companies are not simply doing lip service to this idea because they have actually seen results of the raised awareness and the positive outcomes of diversifying workforces. Even though there is a lot more work to be done in this area, there is definitely a trend of more and more opportunities opening up for a wider range of people now than ever before.

If your dream job still feels out of reach, what are some stepping-stone positions that would get you closer to that dream?

While reaching out to people, do as much research as you can. What are they doing, what are their interests, what are they posting about? What have they been quoted in the press for? Stu Heinecke had a few nuggets to add here. When I asked him for examples of how he thinks outside the box he offered:

Whatever it is—their hot button—it might be that they are going to go on Sir Richard Branson's own spaceflight—it could be anything—then I'd send them a model of the spacecraft. Something I mean, just something that creates a human-to-human connection. And I think that would be hugely in my favor because the top people would be saying, this is the kind of initiative and audacity I'm looking for across our team! You need to demonstrate that, and you don't get to demonstrate that from just a resume.

* * * *

Career pivoting is more common today due to changing work culture, technological advancements and most importantly the fact that we all are craving more satisfaction from a job than just money to pay the bills. If there is a job you've been dreaming about for years, you owe it to yourself to reach for that goal.

Are You Ready to Pivot?

1. Work with your career coach to hone in on passions and skills you have which you are not currently monetizing. Research whether people are making a good living using those skills.
2. Rate yourself on the scale of 1–10 and ask others if they are willing to pay you for those skills. Build your branding assets using your skill. It can be your website or blog or testimonials from people who may be willing, or who are already paying for those services from you.
3. If you are in a financial position to leave your current job and pivot, then go all out for it. Otherwise, is there a side hustle you can work at while you begin a career pivot?

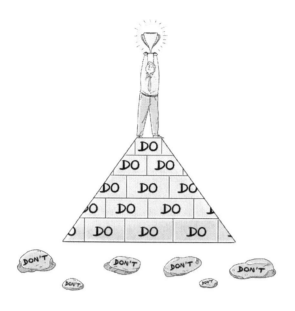

SO, YOU WANT TO BE AN ENTREPRENEUR

"I'm convinced that about half of what separates the successful entrepreneurs from the non-successful ones is pure perseverance."

~ Steve Jobs

MY DEFINITION OF entrepreneurship is identifying an opportunity to do something new or better that only you can do best and having the tenacity and plan to execute on it. What will this path look like for you? It all depends. It starts when you have an idea, you've done some research, and you're sure your passion will carry you through. If you're open-minded, resilient, and you feel you've got true grit, read on!

There are dozens, maybe hundreds of books out there telling you how to become an entrepreneur. If you are reading one that says there is only one way to do things, toss that one out! While it's true that some people who are successful entrepreneurs have MBAs from Columbia or the Wharton School of Business, there are also teenagers who have turned their TikTok channel or Instagram into "influencer" empires. Luccas Neto is a twenty-eight-year-old whose family-friendly videos enabled him to create a thirty-three million-viewer YouTube channel.

One of the most rewarding aspects of becoming an entrepreneur for me was not just creating a business to sustain my family, but also creating hundreds of jobs for other people. Job creators can have an incredibly positive impact on the people who work for them, their families, and the greater society. It feels great to this day knowing that I had a positive impact with those companies and continue to have a positive impact with Mom Relaunch.

The purpose of this chapter is not to tell you how to get rich quickly, nor is it to send you off to get an MBA. With my own entrepreneurial lessons as a backdrop, I will give you my best advice on developing the mindset, support, and framework to become successful on your entrepreneurial journey.

Like David Heinemeier Hansson, I also consider myself to be the counter melody. When I started out, I had no business degree, and I still don't have one today. In fact, I never even aspired to be an entrepreneur. Looking back, I can say that I stumbled onto that path because I recognized a rare opportunity. I understood that the service I provided was not being done better by anyone else. What turned me into an entrepreneur was not giving myself an excuse to let go of the opportunity in front of me. Though I had many constraints to deal with, I made it work. Believing in myself was the only thing I had, and I took a leap of faith and never looked back.

One thing all entrepreneurs would agree on is that running a business is like a game of whack-a-mole—you never know what will pop out next! This definitely is not the path of guaranteed security. "Never a dull moment," most definitely applies to the entrepreneurial path. Now you can explore your options and plan in a safe, judgment-free environment that will help you determine your next moves.

Traits of an Entrepreneur

There are definitive traits an entrepreneur needs to have, and whether or not these come naturally, they should be cultivated as you continue on this path. This is not a predictable path, so the only non-negotiable trait is being agile and nimble, ready to confront challenges as they come up, and pivot as necessary.

- Open-mindedness

Everything you do has to mold itself to what the customer wants because, without them, your business falls apart. In Part Two of the book, we often spoke about remaining relevant. This is especially important for entrepreneurs. Remember that the only constant is change. Most of us get in our comfort zone if the business is doing well and we become so wrapped up in running the day-to-day operations that we forget to zoom out and adapt to incipient changes on the horizon. Don't make this mistake. Always have your finger on both the pulse of trends in your industry as well as on your customers' wants and needs.

- Tenacity

If you give up easily, or have a ready store of excuses you practice, or blame someone for your failure then entrepreneurship is not the right path for you. The buck stops with you the business owner. If you don't have the strength to continually retool and brainstorm solutions, you will become frustrated and you will eventually come to understand you made the wrong choice by heading down this path.

- Be decisive

You will have advice from trusted people in your inner circle, and you may be devouring information from every blog and internet guru out there, that's fine. It is very easy for people, even advisors, to make suggestions, but bear in mind these suggestions may be difficult to execute for your business for whatever reason, especially if you are a solo bootstrapped business. Keep your receiving antennas on but learn how to filter so you can distinguish valuable advice from noise. At the end of the day, you must trust your own judgment and be decisive.

- Know your strengths, know your weaknesses

So many people spend a great deal of time trying to get better at the things that do not come naturally to them. I say don't waste your energy there. Lean into your strengths. Hire great people to do the tasks you're unsuited for. This does not mean hiring super-expensive people. Get creative. Find an underdog who needs a chance, perhaps a stay-at-home parent who wants to reenter the workforce. One of the best developers I ever hired is from the Ukraine. I took a chance on him and he over delivered—in fact, I would say his work is the reason behind the high quality and superfast release of our products.

Building a business is a massive undertaking that can feel overwhelming at times. Fortunately, the basic rule of problem solving applies to running a business—break the problem down into smaller, more manageable chunks. Baby steps, one foot after the other until the problem is no more.

Let's go over these steps here, keeping in mind that there's *never* enough time, money, or other resources to build a successful business. We will focus on how to use all these constraints to your advantage, in the hopes that this will make you more aware and more focused on utilizing everything you already have more effectively.

Go Back to Your Storyboard

Refer to the story you wrote in the first section. Reacquaint yourself with your "why." How does that story relate to this business you're starting? If you can't find an answer, please redo your story. Find the reason why you are passionate about starting this business and what will make you successful. Practice telling your story multiple times to multiple people and analyze their responses. Test the market by seeing if they would buy the product or service you will be building based on your story.

Ask yourself some pointed questions:

- How does your current brand you have personally help you with your business?
- Are you a subject matter expert in your field?
- Can you build a business around your knowledge?
- Why does your product or service matter?
- How is your product a fit for the market?
- Why have larger companies not been able to fill this need?
- Why would you be able to do something better than a large company?

You may not be a known brand in your field but if you are comfortable that you have the knowledge to do something better than competitors in the space, you are on the right track.

Jen Sargent mentioned following two compelling reasons for starting her business:

- She found a gap that she felt she had the skills to address and better than the competition
- She did not like the bureaucratic structure of the company she was working for

Negative Visualization

This may sound like a real downer, so let me explain. Many coaches, gurus, and guides out there accentuate the importance of bringing positivity to everything you do. I agree. But rather than believing in pie in the sky, you must let reality guide you.

There's a stoic technique called negative visualization—you'll recall I wrote about in the last chapter. Imagine that you started a business, invested everything you had, and the business failed. I had an opportunity to interview Day Veerlapati, CEO of S2Tech in St. Louis about how he got over the fear of failure.

I had to ensure that if I die because of business stress/heart attack, then my wife, and kids are taken care of. I looked at my last social security statement. When I felt that if the worst ever happens, my wife and kids all can go back to India and still be able to live on social security survivor benefit, it gave me strength to march forward.

If you do that work upfront, the negative visualization can help you anticipate problems by backtracking to reflect on what went wrong. Imagine that you spent two years building this business and no one wanted to buy your product. How would that make you feel? What would you have to change? How will you go about making those changes? Should you take on less risk? Should you do things differently? Should it take three years instead of two? Expect failure so that you might actually avoid failing.

Ideation

What is your business idea? Why do you think people will buy from you? Have you spoken with anyone objective and had this idea validated? Who have you spoken with to validate this? If you reply, "My mom and my aunt," that might be okay, moms and aunts are awesome, but you should broaden your scope and talk to more people! Do you know what your ideal customer looks like? There is only one way to find this out, and that is by talking to your potential customers first. Reach out to them, interview them, dig deep into their problems. How are you planning to solve these problems? Is this customer buying from you every time or is he or she doing you a favor by buying from you because you are a friend?

It is critical to empathize with your customers and think like them, to feel what it's like to be in their shoes. When I started my software business, my first line of sales used to be that I know what it is to run a staffing company given that I used to own one. Whatever solution I'm providing is trying to solve the main problems every staffing company faces. That's the time I use to gain the confidence and trust of my potential customers.

Whatever your idea is, make sure the solution is customer-centric.

And though having a passion for the idea you want to develop is one important ingredient for success, it's not the whole recipe. Anuradha Basu, Professor of Entrepreneurship, San Jose State University speaks very strongly about this point.

Entrepreneurs are always passionate about their idea. But if they are going to be successful, they have to create that same passion in others.

Unless you are operating in a vacuum, chances are someone out there also has a similar idea to yours. Don't panic. The old saying, "Imitation is the sincerest form of flattery" should ring true enough that you're not surprised. Anu talks about this very concept with her students, but she takes it a step further:

You should feel really vindicated if someone actually steals your idea. But that also shows that you're slow at implementing it and someone has beaten you to it!

Remember, there is more than one marketing company, more than one software developer, more than one wellness coach. Don't be daunted by the fact that others are out there in your arena. Competition is healthy, it's a good measuring stick. You have to remember that although someone has a business similar to yours, your perspective, talent, experience, and energy make yours a unique offering. Focus on adding value to your customers' lives and you will be on the right track.

The Right Idea at the Right Time

Being aware of the business climate and having a finger on the pulse of the culture is key when you are thinking of starting up a venture. You would not think to open up an indie bookstore down the street from Barnes and Noble, nor would you open up a boutique or a dry-cleaning business during a global pandemic.

When I asked Jen Sargent more specifically about the impetus for starting her company, HitFix, she spoke about the climate being right, and how her idea was a unique offering:

At the time, everything was very segmented between movies and TV, and music. But times were changing and there was a lot of intermingling. So, the premise was really a new digital media company for entertainment. Hitfix was an entertainment news brand focused on helping consumers discover, talk about, and experience movies, music, TV, and pop culture through the lens of insiders.

In some respects, the timing was not perfect. This was 2008, in the shadow of the Great Recession, but Jen was able to raise funding and then grow Hitfix for eight years until it was acquired by Uproxx Media Group in 2016.

In hindsight, I can easily see that I chose absolutely crazy times to start my businesses! My first company started in mid-2002 right after 9/11. My second company started in 2008 right when the market meltdown was happening. My third company, Mom Relaunch, launched just before a global pandemic that no one saw coming. The lesson here is that every business, new or existing, must learn to adapt to the times. When you find a way to bring value and create a necessary service, you may find that even in lean and challenging times your business can thrive.

How Will You Generate Revenue?

Do you know what your customers are willing to pay for your products or services? If not then it's research time, budding entrepreneur. Come up with a pricing strategy that works for your user base. Your goal is not to just get into a pricing battle with your competitors. You need to be creating a pricing model based on the value your company can provide, and you can't do that if you don't know how much that market will bear.

Repeat business will be essential for building a clientele, so no matter what you are selling, work hard to find a way to build customer loyalty. This can involve loyalty programs, memberships, or referral rewards. Creating an engaged customer base should be part of your pricing strategy. These are the customers who will become your evangelists, the rocket fuel that supercharges your business. One tweet or post from someone with thousands of followers can do wonders for your exposure.

Be prepared to change the revenue model as you grow your business. You may also have to go through different pricing iterations in order to find the sweet spot.

Identify Your Entrepreneurial Style

There are two types of people needed for a successful business—the creator and the marketer. I always use the two Steves analogy here.

- Steve Jobs – Visionary and Marketer – Has the vision for the product and communicates that vision to others.
- Steve Wozniak – Creator – Can implement the vision as a sellable product or service.

What is your type? Refer to the characteristics you wrote down when completing the exercise in the Core Competencies chapter. Refer also to your alignment framework to help answer these questions. Which Steve are you? You'll need to either hire or partner with the other Steve. Or you'll need to hire someone as a consultant before you start. It's fine to learn as you go, but if you are not confident that you can serve both roles then put some effort into finding your counter-ballast. In my case, I was serving both functions, but deep down I always felt that it would have been better to have someone else take one of the roles.

Solo vs. Partnership

It is highly recommended to have a co-founder or co-founders who can fill in where you are not as strong. You may have heard the saying, "Show me your friends and I will show you your future." This is true at every age, and in every aspect of life. Getting the right partner can make or break your business, so take time to find the right person. In many respects, choosing a business partner is like choosing a life partner because so many of your dealings will be enmeshed. If you have to end a partnership, it can be like a complex divorce. So, enter with your eyes open and do extensive vetting.

- Just as you did in the Network chapter, make a list of people who have done something similar to your area of expertise and achieved success. List why you might want to reach out to them. Categorize them in terms of how difficult they are to reach.

- Have an outreach plan for them—warm referrals or cold emails

- Figure out what's in it for them should they join you and then make an irresistible offer

- If you are having difficulty doing this on your own, you can hire someone to find a co-founder for you or join programs that help find a match

Advisory Board

I use this term loosely, referring to those trusted few people who are in your corner. These are people who are willing to go the extra mile to help you succeed, even if that means giving their time every now and then to hear you out and help you weigh your options. Reach out to the personal board of advisors/mentors you've curated and work with them to help you achieve your potential. Work out financials with them—if possible *pro bono* with some equity down the line. While I never had anyone formally in this role, I was lucky to have several people who I fondly refer to as friends of the company who were instrumental in giving their advice at critical junctures.

Advisory board members should:

- Be very candid and vocalize their opinions
- Bring accountability and help take your ego out of the decision-making process
- Be open to introducing you to their network
- Complement you in the areas where you are not as strong

Cart before the Horse

You must have a committed customer before you even register your company. Sounds contrary to logic, right? But I did this successfully for each company I started, and it was a formula that worked.

To start with, have a very clear concept of your customer's pain points. How is your product/service going to solve their problem? It's critical to keep ahead of the competition with a product that is not just going to solve a little problem but is something truly essential with legs to grow. And the only way you can understand whether you are building something truly essential is from your customers.

In an Inc article called "11 Ways to Get Your First 1,000 Customers,"[45] Mitch Wainer, CMO of DigitalOcean, provides some

---

45 https://www.inc.com/christina-desmarais/11-ways-to-get-your-first-1000-users-and-beyond.html?utm_source=zapier.com&utm_medium=referral&utm_campaign=zapier

great tips on acquiring and understanding early adopters. Wainer says, "DigitalOcean attracted its first fifty customers by demoing in front of a New York tech meetup. However, you capture your first cadre of users, make sure to offer whatever you're creating or building for free in beta, and then learn from your mistakes as quickly as possible. 'Fail faster' is the motto, and that's going to allow you to adjust and find the success stories and work within those success stories. You want to learn as much as possible about your first hundred users in the beginning."

In my experience, having a customer before you launch not only reduces your risk, it brings you peace of mind.

Register Your Business and Website Domain

Now that you have your co-founder in place if you decide to have one, your idea is validated, you have your advisory board, and most importantly your first customer in place, you can register your company and be in business. Choose wisely when you come up with a business name. Pick something unique and memorable (with an available URL).

Patent Your Product

Once you have decided on your company concept, brand, and name, start the process of trademarking and patenting it. There are several ways to do this, but, speaking from experience, you should consider finding a good lawyer who specializes in this area. Nowadays there are legal services that are provided on a subscription basis that can help you get started at a very low cost, but this is one expense I would justify. I recommend finding a reputed law firm that is willing to work with you on some flexible payment terms. Negotiate hard! You can start working on your legal documents like an NDA and client contracts and have them ready to go.

Finances

Deciding how to fund your business is one of the biggest issues you will need to get right. With all the glamour and media attention around startups and VCs, it's important to keep in mind that bootstrapping a business the old-fashioned way is still a great option for a new venture.

Fortunately, in the last several years, the price of operating a business has decreased significantly. Business operations have been democratized. The tools and technology that were once only available to big firms are now available to all. As I mentioned in earlier chapters, the global pandemic of 2020 not only forced businesses to operate remotely, it also shined a light on the fact that operating remotely offers a great deal of freedom and lowers overhead for business owners. There are dozens of excellent software options for teams collaborating on projects together that remove the need for everyone to meet in person.

Do You Need Funding?

Naeem Zafar, a Berkeley Business School professor, explains it very simply by categorizing business in the following ways:

1. Time-sensitive

If you are in a competitive business and you are racing to get your product to market, time is of the essence. If you don't drive fast, somebody else will win. In this case, you can think about raising external funds, giving up some equity and control to buy the time to expedite starting up your business. Most of the companies that fall into this category are those that come up with a brand-new idea or find an innovative way to work on an existing idea. It is essential in this case to get the maximum number of customers as soon as possible.

2. Taking the long view. (Done is better than perfect)

This is for marathoners rather than sprinters. In this case, deal with your financial constraints, bootstrap and do the best you can when you're starting out. Focus on doing what you can do with the cash you have on hand. This is a great exercise to force yourself to take a hard look at what's really essential to purchase and what you can do without. If you are planning to build a product, focus on the minimal functionality necessary to get the product out the door and generate revenue. You can always iterate along the way, enhance the product, and streamline operations.

3. Hybrid

There are some well-run, profitable bootstrapped companies who choose to raise external funds after being in business for several years. This may be for any number of reasons, including the desire to expand.

A Breakdown of Funding Options

Let's take a closer look at three broad categories: bootstrapping, professional funding, and grants and loans.

1. Bootstrapping a business means you are either starting out with what you have, using your own savings, leveraging a credit card, or borrowing from friends and family to get your

business off the ground. When you bootstrap a business, the rewards can be great, but the tradeoff is that you must figure everything out as you go. You may hustle harder, work more hours, and wear many different hats as a bootstrapped start-up. You may not have enough money to attract the talent you want to hire.

Running the finances of a bootstrapped business is a lot like managing your own personal finances. Many people choose to start a company while they are still working at a job. There is nothing wrong with this, but it will limit how quickly you can get your business off the ground. If possible, you should try to work as a consultant so that your hours are more flexible, allowing for you to devote time to your own venture. Ideally, the consulting work you do is in the same arena you are building a business around, because this way you not only have a steady income you gain valuable real-world experience in the process. You can see firsthand what your customers' pain points are, and possibly even convert your consulting clients when you're ready to launch.

Borrowing from family and friends has its own pros and cons. When money is involved, relationships can get tricky. Things tend to go well when business is good but losing family money can impact your relationship. So, before you take this path, make sure you've worked with friends and relatives on the negative visualization, and confirmed that if things don't work out the failure won't torpedo the relationship.

If you can manage to grow your business to your satisfaction by bootstrapping, I think this is the best option. You get the best valuation on exit, and it's a very satisfying experience achieving something on your own and being your own boss.

2. Professional funding – Angels and VCs

We live in a culture where fundraising is celebrated and glamorized, so we need to keep it real here. It's no small thing impressing an investor and getting them on board. Many businesses need to raise capital in order to gain market share at the earliest possible time.

One key thing you need to understand is that the moment you bring in investors, you are no longer your own boss with your own singular vision. You will now be under pressure to satisfy the interests of your investors.

Angel investors are generally wealthy individuals who were entrepreneurs themselves. If you decide to go this route, make a list of all angel groups, especially ones that have previously invested in your domain. If they don't fund you for whatever reason, you might still get good advice from the group and some members may even join your venture as a mentor. If you find an angel who wants to invest, he or she will usually invest in you for the following reasons:

- They see something of themselves in you and want to help you succeed
- They are subject matter experts in your business and can add value as an advisor
- They love your idea and see the potential of multiplying their investments through your company

Venture Capitalists (VCs) collect money from different sources and operate as a group seeking business opportunities that can make their investments grow to great returns. Their goal is to make money for their investors and generally invest large amounts of money in the company. They work with the owners to find an exit strategy that will give the investors gains on their investment. Keep in mind that having an exit is very important to the VC because that's how they make money. Exits can happen by selling the company through merger or acquisition or going IPO where shares are floated in the stock market. If you get involved with VC money, keep the following in mind:

- VC money is considered risk money. They do a very thorough analysis of your business to determine how and when they can get their money back. They take substantial risk in investing without much collateral or other safety nets.
- They can also provide guidance and advice along the way if they choose to. They have seen and done this before so it's always beneficial to ask them to help in every capacity if you can.
- Only about 6% of businesses are funded by VC money, so bear this in mind if you are going after this type of investment.

You may be wondering what is different about the startups that are funded by angel investors and venture capitalists. Why do they receive funding while thousands of thousands of others do not?

When I asked Tim Draper, a successful VC in Silicon Valley, he explained the criteria in very simple terms.

I look for entrepreneurs who can't help but do what they are doing. As a startup, they should get something into their customer's hands as soon as they can. The best entrepreneurs have a grand vision but consider delighting their customers every step of the way. Before I meet with them, I consider their plan and whether it is

1. *Big enough in market size*
2. *Unique enough in technology, and*
3. *Has the right team to execute the vision*

Successful funding often comes down to networking. For VC investments, many of the startups are founded by second or third-time entrepreneurs. These are people who have previously raised money from venture capitalists. Ultimately, investors are trusting the entrepreneur with their money, and thus, underneath the whole process, a relationship needs to be created. All of this boils down to the old adage, *who you know is more important than what you know.*

Though the stories of a $1 million investment turned into $100 million get a great deal of media attention, they are the rare exception. All glamour and drama aside, the vast majority of entrepreneurs manage to get their business up and running without any angel or venture capital funding, using savings, loans from friends and family, and little else in terms of funding.

3. Grants and Loans

A business grant is monetary funding from the government or an organization that is given in order to help small businesses and nonprofits. Unlike loans, you don't have to pay this money back. There's no collateral that you're required to put up, and you won't need to pay fees or interest. While small business owners may dream of receiving grants to fund their startup, they may not be as plentiful or easy to get as you may think. However, if you know where to look and how to apply, you might be successful in securing free money for your business. While grant money is awarded to you, it may come with rules that dictate how you can spend it. Once you find the grant that you think is best for your business, gather everything you need to know before applying. Understand what's required in the application, when it's due, and anything else that may be needed.

Be aware that a grant application might require an outline of your proposed work and financial data on your organization. Be sure to follow the parameters of the grant application and don't leave anything out. If you're feeling intimidated by the application, consider bringing in another party to help you fill it out. If you need help, check out the grant-writing classes, conferences, workshops, and other resources out there.

Another option is hiring an experienced grant writer to develop your startup business grant proposals for you. No matter how you approach the process, the rewards are there for small business owners who put in the time and energy to submit a complete and compelling grant proposal.

Product and Services

Whether you are providing a product or a service, it is critical to have an agile mindset and to quickly deliver a quality solution into the hands of the customers. There are two different approaches here. My approach to product development was a super-fast, agile method. There was not much process or sanity around it, but we kept our focus on one critical thing—customer feedback and suggestions.

The other school of thought, often referred to as the Steve Jobs way, is to refrain from asking customers what they want because they may not be sure. There is a famous quote attributed to Henry Ford: "If I had asked people what they wanted, they would have said faster horses." Customers can easily describe a problem they're having—in this case, wanting to get somewhere faster—but not the best solution.

I never invested time and money in doing market research, talking to analysts, or utilizing typical software development methodologies. We simply heard our customers' needs and provided them solutions. It was as simple as that.

Marketing

Most companies do not spend enough time and money marketing their products and services. Many people are intimidated by the idea of hiring big, reputable ad agencies, but remember thanks to social media, SEO, and the blogosphere, these days there exists a wealth of excellent marketing avenues for a small budget. Growing an audience beyond your core people is an essential next step.

Teresa Lagerman of Condensed advises: "*Establishing a strong brand is the best investment a startup can make. Smart marketing can help legitimize a new company, create excitement, and engage potential clients. Nobody knows you yet, so you need to get people to care enough to try what you offer.*"[46]

When you create a website, offer content that will build your reputation as a results leader. Don't just plug your products and services—a lot of what digital marketing encompasses is tangential content. What is tangential content, you may be wondering? This is stuff that provides value for your customers, even if it's not directly related to your brand. For example, a travel agency might publish a post highlighting the best restaurants to eat in Los Angeles, since that is a popular destination city.

This gets the reader to see the connection between the content and the brand. In this case, the post showcases where the customer can go if they use your travel agency. Tangential content does three things:

1. Helps your brand build its reputation
2. Improves link building, reaches more people
3. Increases audience engagement

Put to use all you learned in the *You as a Brand* chapter. Establishing yourself as a results leader inspires trust and authority—it will be the reason you connect with your customers and get them to try your product or service.

---

[46] https://condensed.io/

Sales

Getting meetings in all forms is at the center of getting anything done, and Stu Heinecke had some excellent out-of-the-box tactics to get people's attention in his book, *How to Get a Meeting with Anyone*. Just as he advised in the networking chapter to go for it and be creative with your "reach" contacts, you should also be clever with approaching people you want to do business with as an entrepreneur.

I was inspired by Stu's story about starting up his marketing business. He became famous for what he calls "contact marketing," a uniquely human process of making an impression on someone you want to get a meeting with the old-fashioned way. When he thought about how to break through to two dozen critically important prospects with a near 100% success rate, this is what he came up with:

Since the audience was so small, I could afford to budget more per person while spending far less than what a marketer typically does on a campaign. So, I produced a set of twenty-four prints, each suitable for framing and featuring a cartoon personalized with the recipient's name and sent it with a letter.

My total spend was less than $100, but I reached and sold to all of my targets. Suddenly, my small freelance business had a roster of clients that included Time, Inc, Forbes, Harvard Business Review, The Wall Street Journal, Conde Nast, and Hearst Magazines, all paying up to $25,000 per assignment. I've never calculated the cost/return ratio on that early contact campaign, but it is surely in the millions of percent.

Remember two things:

1. Nothing ventured, nothing gained
2. Chutzpah!

Team Building

Just as it is important to empathize with your customers, it is equally as important to empathize with your team members. If your employees are happy then your customers will be happy. Create a positive work culture where curiosity, collaboration, and innovation are encouraged. When everyone feels like they're part of a mission, then everyone from the assistants on up to the head of the company can take pride in creating an excellent product that is adding value to the world.

As a founder, my philosophy was to always take the long view and hire people with an eye towards giving them a career, and not just a job. This ended up working out very nicely, in fact, many of our core team members from those early days are still with us today. I would rather train someone with the right attitude than take someone on who has the skills but lacks the team mentality.

Another thing to consider when hiring is that with all the advances in technology, the best people for the job don't necessarily have to be regional. An international team adds great diversity and removes any kind of physical limitations. It's also great to have a mix of both younger and more experienced people so that your team has a broad perspective.

I never had a formal process of creating performance reviews and other typical HR-related processes, however, my doors were always open for everyone to come and talk to me. They all knew that we have family-friendly policies that value work-life harmony. One very popular move that I made was giving every employee a paid day off to celebrate the day they came into this world! No one should work on his/her birthday.

Channel Partners

If you are a small, bootstrapped company, you may want to align yourself with a channel partner. Think of all the terrain we covered in the *Professional Ecosystem* chapter. When you take advantage of a platform that is already established, it brings instant trustworthiness and legitimacy to your business. In the ecosystem chapter, I wrote about the success I had early on, which would not have been possible if I hadn't partnered with Salesforce.

My mentor, Mike Kreaden, explains the beginnings of the Salesforce ecosystem, and how the early developers actually had no idea how powerful a platform this would become for both the users and the creators.

In the space of two years, we went from thinking we need to support what would be an ecosystem of apps. Now, at that point, we weren't even envisioning that we would get past a few hundred apps, let alone thousands. And it was just a means to an end. But very quickly, I think that as soon as early 2007, we realized that there was a bigger opportunity here. And the ecosystem itself grew out of what we were already doing with our community.

Focus on Profitability

I summarize my success as a bootstrapped founder in one line—I never lost sleep worrying how I would make my next payroll. I always had twelve months of cash flow and only one metric to track—are we profitable every month? In the current business zeitgeist, there is an overabundance of emphasis on fundraising and spending money on growth when founders and investors should be focusing on profit. While I do understand that not all businesses can be profitable early on, I suggest you never lose sight of this very critical aspect of entrepreneurialism. In business and life, we should not spend more than we earn. Or as Clay Christensen of Harvard Business School has said, "Be impatient for profits, and patient for growth."

Speaking with a serial entrepreneur friend about the delicate balance between profitability and growth, he said, "*I always say my number one rule of entrepreneurship is no matter whatever else happens, don't ever, ever run out of cash. I've always been skeptical of companies that have chased growth at the expense of self-sufficiency.*"

The Pursuit of Happiness

Ironically, in the pursuit of avoiding the hamster wheel of the corporate world, many entrepreneurs recreate a stressful, crazy pace and can't see (or enjoy) the forest for the trees. When I asked my friend about how entrepreneurs can decide when enough is enough his response was:

I think that's a great question, especially because we live in such a materialistic society and that makes it hard to identify. For me, there is a sense of self-satisfaction that comes from knowing that my basic needs and the basic needs of the people I love are cared for. And then any excess over that goes into the bucket of happiness.

The same can be said for being happy in your business by knowing that you are meeting your needs and those of your employees and customers. Bringing value to your customers gives your company a purpose beyond profit and that meaning will make you happy.

* * * *

Keep in mind that your mindset and your values dictate how the company will be run, so start fresh with a realistic pace, and don't let your three-legged stool get out of balance.

Prepare Yourself for Your Entrepreneurial Journey

1. What's your business idea? Have you canvassed your potential customers to understand their pain points and why your product/service stands out to them? Can you get a written commitment from a potential customer to buy as soon as your product/service is ready?

2. Write down a very high-level business plan for 1–3 years with the focus on finances, customer retention, and hiring a good team. Assume that none of these work out. What is your back-up plan?

3. Will you still be ok emotionally, financially, and socially if nothing works out as planned? Can you move on with your life with a smile on your face with more courage and knowledge to do better next time?

REACH YOUR POTENTIAL IN A TRADITIONAL JOB

Far and away the best prize that life offers is the chance to work hard at work worth doing.

~ Theodore Roosevelt

WHETHER YOU ARE making a vertical change, a horizontal/lattice change, or looking to work in a similar role at a different company, take all the critical work you've done honing your work style, core competencies, and personal brand and go forward with intention to find the job that is going to bring you a feeling of happiness and success. In this chapter, we are going to talk about all the resources to avail ourselves of, and strategies we can employ to make that happen.

An illuminating 2017 study by Deloitte concluded that only 13% of the workforce are passionate about their jobs. That is not a good recipe for a balanced three-legged stool. Even if you need to take a position that is not ideal, you should use this interim period to get clear on where you want to end up, and what stepping-stones you'll need to traverse to get there. Remember that a career is a marathon. Run each leg of the race giving it all you've got, and you'll reach your goal.

Vertical/Ladder Change

A ladder career change simply means moving up the corporate chain either in your existing company or in a similar organization in your industry. This indicates that you have developed deep subject matter expertise and are ready for the challenge. Promotions come with a higher salary and a better title to flaunt. They may also come with some management and leadership responsibilities, depending on the job.

Horizontal/Lattice Change

A lattice job change allows you to make changes in your role and responsibilities in a new area, in a different department either in your own company or another company within the same industry. You may be attracted to making a move like this either because you want to expand your skills or find a position that better suits your lifestyle. As you may recall from the *Parental Indecision* chapter, Kim Sneeder was very happy making a lateral move that allowed her to achieve a lifestyle that was more conducive to starting a family.

This decision can be very tough to make if you have an option to go up the ladder with potentially more obvious benefits. Once again, go back to your core competencies and most importantly your alignment framework to help you decide based on your vision and values for yourself at this time. If you're feeling financial pressure, you may consider a part-time job while you devote yourself to finding a good fit. Mara Swan, President of Xceleration LLC and HR industry expert, had a lot of experience working with job seekers in her role with Right Management, a company that provided career services. I asked her about the concern of money worries and how that can play into one's decision process, she said, *"When people are under financial pressure, all plans go for a toss, however, this is a critical time to assess all aspects of their work and life to make the right decision."*

Job Hunting Is a Full-Time Job

You must place all of your focus on your job search to plan and execute it well. The key is to have accountability, visibility, tracking, and measurement of your job search activities. On a deeper level, it's time to take out your workbook and think about what these jobs have to offer you and put yourself in the driver's seat.

To begin, make a list of companies that you would love to work for. Go to the career section of their website to check for openings that sound interesting to you. These are constantly updated, so be sure to check back often. This is a great way to proactively go after what you want. Think of who you know at that company, or if you do not know anyone, perhaps someone in your network knows someone who can make a connection for you. Check local job boards, search for your job title in an online search engine. Network with any professional contacts who either work for your target company or know somebody there.

Refer to the Job search template[47], make a copy of it to use for your job search. It will help keep track of companies you have reached out to and organize which ones responded, which ones you met with, and also it will give you an indication of interview areas to improve. Keep as detailed notes as possible. If you prefer to track your job search data in another format, just make sure it is well-organized.

Network *(Yes, again!)*

No one will know your desire/intention to make a move unless you proactively express an interest. Once you have a specific goal set, consider who you need to speak with to help you make a career move. If you have a friend in a different department or another company where you would like to work, take your friend out to lunch, and express your intention. People are usually more than willing to help make connections, especially if you have demonstrated competence and earned the respect of your colleagues. Friends and colleagues can spread the word, so your intention gets amplified. Follow up on any leads as soon as possible. Applying all the networking strategies we discussed in earlier chapters is a great way to reach out if you don't know anyone personally in the company where you would like to work.

---

[47] https://docs.google.com/spreadsheets/d/1LBsQq6FJm4aF-qPVo0nmF8MQA_NJQ0jCXUY7XPEZPWA/edit#gid=740332029

Leverage Your Current Employer

If you have a good relationship with your current employer/supervisor, let them know that you are exploring other opportunities. Explain your current situation as clearly as possible, especially if you are consciously uncoupling from your job. If your company really values your talent, then they will try to work out some way to keep you. This opens up the door to have conversations with people within the organization to try to find a good fit for you.

Remember not to burn the bridge with your current employer, you never know when you may need help from them. Never badmouth your current employer on social media or any public platform. When you speak about them in interviews with prospective employers, use non-incendiary language. Frame the conversation in a positive light—if there was a lack of compatibility, not enough challenges, and you felt like you weren't able to make a difference, express that that is what you are looking for at your next job.

Lean into Your Transferable Skills

We have touched on transferable skills once or twice as they relate to re-entering the workforce, but in the case of a lateral career move, transferable skills are also critical. Your biggest transferable skill here is knowing the work culture and being established in the organization. Your expertise in one position may very well carry over to other positions, and your soft skills definitely come into play here. If you are valued at the organization for your analytical skills, team building, communication, teamwork, time management, creative thinking, and conflict resolution, you have already demonstrated your value in more than one way.

If you are looking to get hired at a new company, it's even more imperative to demonstrate that you have what it takes in terms of job familiarity and soft skills.

If there is a position you are interested in going after, consider which transferable skills make you a fit for this position. These are things you can play up when discussing the position with your supervisor, or the contact at the company where you plan to apply.

Professional Development

Demonstrate that you are willing and eager to learn any new skills you may need to acquire before changing positions. If there is a way to get a head start on this by doing some training, shadowing, courses, or volunteer work, show that you are open to doing whatever it takes to get the position you want.

In regard to transferable skills, remember that banking more skills now is a great thing for the future. Every job brings new challenges, so even if your new job has many of the same responsibilities as your old job, you will be learning new systems and capabilities that you will take with you on your next move. So even if you haven't made a huge jump in pay, this job may be a stepping stone to ultimately get you closer to your end goal.

Polish Your Resume

Preparing a good resume is an art. Thinking about summarizing your professional experience in a two-page document can be a stressful task especially when you know that very likely, it will be filtered by a machine before it reaches human eyes. Mara Swan talked about how people in her generation were taught to look for talent and read resumes to see the human behind the paper. Yes, it can be daunting knowing that some level of electronic screening goes on, but there are ways around that. All you can do is be as authentic as possible in writing up your resume, and then be proactive in getting it in the hands of the right people. Keep in mind these tips to perfect your resume:

- Customize resumes to fit the job. No matter how good your resume is, it cannot be a fit for all the jobs you are applying for. Take keywords from the job description and put them in your resume. That's the first trick in putting your resume on the radar of machine recruiters.
- Highlight skills that are relevant to the job.
- Use numbers and accomplishments to showcase the impact of your work in your current jobs.
- Handle resume gaps creatively. Try to put some titles for those years. Many women we train in our program make the mistake of not acknowledging the skills they gained during a career break volunteering for schools, liaising between groups, fundraising, running committees and projects. When you list your accomplishments during a career break it serves 3 purposes:
  - It minimizes the glaring break
  - It shows confidence in your skills and opens up an opportunity to discuss the break should you be asked about it
  - You're not hiding anything, and you're not guilty about stepping away for a worthwhile reason. Mara echoed this sentiment: "*People tend to want to make excuses, like they almost feel guilty for taking a career break. So, they're over explaining it, and it takes away from their overall skills. I think you have to go in with utmost confidence.*" Her

advice: *simply state what you did professionally in the past, and that you took a career break because it was what was best for your family.*

Write a Knockout Cover Letter

The cover letter is a chance to introduce yourself and sell yourself beyond just skills. This is where you show your passion for this area of work. However, it's crucial you do your homework. As Scott Gordon points out that it's a big mistake to copy a generic form letter off the internet. As a recruiter, he is looking for genuine interest and specificity.

Be specific with the client. Why do you want to work at this company, what about this position interests you? If I get a well-crafted email that is three or four sentences long that says here's why I'm interested in this position, I'm going to pick up the phone and call that candidate back because if they say, I see that you've got a position with Mars Pet Care in Nashville, I'd love to talk to you about my background and database administration. Okay, great. versus just, 'dear hiring manager attached is my resume.

It's also important to strike the right tone—eagerness, passion, and interest are great, but desperation is not a good look on anyone. It will turn prospective employers off.

Video Resumes

I recommend that you create a short video resume of yourself to submit along with your traditional resume. This is a way to showcase your communication skills. It allows you a very personal means of expressing your interest in joining the company. Before you submit it, make sure to check first if the company is accepting video resumes.

Resumes Are Not the Only Thing

It's no secret that most employers do an internet search, look at your social media profiles and not just your resume. We have discussed a lot about this topic in the *You as a Brand* chapter. Investigate how you are going to appear in a Google search—what does it tell your prospective employer that is not in your resume? Be prepared to have an answer if anything objectionable shows up that can affect your chances of getting hired.

In the Lifelong Learning chapter, we talked about how you can track your learning using the Degreed platform. Now you can showcase your knowledge and demonstrate how highly you value learning new skills.

Be Honest and Don't Feel Guilty

The market today is full of fake resumes. There are even resume coaches who will advise you to embellish and get creative with your resume. Unfortunately, the statement, *fake it till you make it* is definitely not applicable to resumes. This is something I have never encouraged in my staffing company or in Mom Relaunch. If you took a career break, own it proudly. If you are truthful in an interview about the reasons behind your break and the experiences you gained during that time, it humanizes you and counts as a positive, not a negative, that you have tried different things and had various life experiences.

Application Submission and Follow Up

Before you apply for a job, find out if you know anyone in that company directly or indirectly. Have a call with that person so you can get an understanding of the company culture. Build a good relationship with them and see if they can become your referral/ally. Some of the companies also offer referral bonuses, so it can be an additional incentive for the person to help you, especially if they think you are a good fit for the company. Follow the company process of application but request your referral to submit your resume through his or her internal channel, if possible.

After you submit an application, make a human connection by reaching out to HR. Most of the time, people in HR are willing to talk to you and give some pointers if you reach out to them. You may not get a response back, but it's quite possible they may remember seeing your follow-up emails and it can help you earn some extra points if you make an impression on the recruiter or hiring manager.

Be an Interview Ninja

If you get an interview call, pat yourself on the back because this means you are among the top 20% of applicants to make the cut. Understanding next steps and how to prepare for them is key to your success.

- Connect with anyone and everyone you can at this company and request them to be your allies. This is definitely not the time to be shy. See if you can get some inside information on company culture and what is expected from employees in this role. Customize your elevator pitch that you created in the networking chapter to match as closely as possible with your skills and also with the company to which you are applying. If you use the right words in your elevator pitch, employers should see that they don't have to train you in the company values and culture as you have already done that work and it shows.

- There is no lack of information about the company on the internet in terms of their website, services that provide ratings about companies, etc. Learn as much as possible about the company and envision yourself in the role. When you are interviewing, act as if you are in that role, prepare to answer in a way that will show the impact you can bring to the company. If you know the person who will be interviewing you, then by all means do your due diligence. Show your respect for their achievements.

- 'Practice makes perfect' is especially true for interviews. Practice by yourself first, record it and continue to make improvements. Then find someone from your network who can take your mock interview and give you honest feedback. Have the courage to listen to any constructive criticism without being hard on yourself. Pick someone for the mock interview who is genuinely interested in your success. You will find there is a lot of free interview preparation help available from career centers, libraries, the internet, and some paid services as well.

- Prepare some questions that you will ask the interviewer. Find the right moment to ask them, it will show that you have done your part and are equally curious about the job as they are to hire someone. Before you end the interview, don't forget to ask when you can hear from them about the next steps and what's the right time frame to follow up.

- During the interview process, both you and the hiring manager/team are looking to find the right fit. It's not just them but you also have to be very vigilant in sussing out whether this is the right job for you. Always remember that an interview is a two-way process so don't sound too needy even if you desperately want to get the job.

As Gwendolyn Turner of Steele and Grace points out, "*This is your opportunity to ask those important questions about the organization—does it fit from a work life balance standpoint? Are they going to respect the fact that my family comes first? And if I have to leave or not be on a zoom call for half a day, will that be accepted?*"

- When it comes to communication, tone and body language speak volumes. It's important to show enthusiasm not only through words but also in your tone and gestures. If the interview is online, make sure you demonstrate focus.

- Send a written thank-you note if possible. This may sound completely old school, but it still works like magic! If you can think of a small thank-you gift that the interviewer may like, it's a good gesture to send it if you can afford it. If possible, something that they can use regularly that will remind them of your conversation.

* * * *

Whether you're looking to move to a different company or staying with the same company, make sure your employer understands that the intention behind your wanting a change is rooted in your passion for your subject matter, and your desire to find the best possible fit so that you can shine in your new position and be a great asset to the organization.

Let's Work on the Job of Finding Your Dream Job

1. Prepare your job search template. Give yourself a deadline. Find someone who can keep you accountable. This should be your mentor/coach and preferably someone who is not part of your family.

2. Make a list of companies you would like to work for and rank them in the order of most desirable to least and apply all the strategies listed above to find allies to help you.

3. Be agile and nimble and continue to improve your strategies based on the learnings you are getting from each step. Nothing is set in stone and something that works for others may not work for you. Be open and creative to see what the best path ahead is.

SUCCEED AS YOUR OWN ONE PERSON ARMY

"If it's meant to be, it's up to me."

~ William Johnsen

A S THE WORLD of work evolves and people navigate the constantly changing terrain, many more fall into the category of "one person army" now than ever. For the sake of clarity, I will refer to gig workers or those who identify as a one-woman/one-man army as freelancers in this chapter.

People who are attracted to freelancing are usually either drawn to the lifestyle it offers or the earning potential, either for a side hustle or a full-time endeavor. Many people are learning that job security is becoming less and less of a "thing" in the current climate. When talking to Barry Asin, President of Staffing Industry Analysts (SIA), he made an important point:

Everyone today is a contingent (temporary) worker, it's just that most of us don't know it.

Of course, when you zoom out and take a spiritual view, we are all on this planet for a short while. All the more reason to be happy and make the best of our situation while we're here.

If you have chosen to freelance, you are a subject matter expert who knows the value you bring and appreciates the freedom of the freelancing lifestyle. Of course, there are pros and cons to freelancing and the term "freedom" is a subjective thing, meaning different things to different people.

The gig economy workforce is growing faster than the overall U.S. workforce. It got its name from the fact that workers are looking for their next gig. However, it's interesting to note that only 7% of the people working in this sector are comfortable with the term "gig economy." Many of them like to call themselves freelancers or small business owners because, for them, it's about building a business, not simply getting their next gig.

Freelancing got its popularity not only from the change in work culture but primarily due to technological advancements. The internet has made it possible for individuals and teams to collaborate on a project even if they are thousands of miles apart. When searching for the right book designer for the cover of our book, I was able to engage Ivica from Croatia through a freelancing platform.

To succeed as a freelancer, you must have the right mindset. First and foremost, you have to take responsibility for your livelihood and your choices because you and only you are accountable for everything. There is no one to help, blame, or do the work for you. If not having a steady income stresses you out, you need to find a traditional job. But if the excitement of new work with new clients appeals to you and you have full belief in your ability to support yourself, then there is no stopping you from charting a successful course for yourself.

If this is your career path for whatever your reasons are, let's look at how to do it right. By now you know what your core competencies are and why are you choosing this path. Going in, you should be clear that you are essentially running a business. The key difference here is that you won't be managing other people. My first suggestion is to refer back to the entrepreneurship chapter because thinking and behaving like an entrepreneur is what you need to do when you are on this path.

Before I delve into the tools and strategies to apply, it's essential you get clear on your motivation. If you are leaving a traditional job to become a one-woman/one-man army, what is your "why?" For Erica Kuhl of EricaKuhl.com, it was something she had been working toward in her mind for a while. When I asked her about her motivation, she said:

I wanted to be the brand and the product I was selling. I have the experience, strategy, frameworks, and relationships. The idea, instead of hiring people, was to scale myself with productizing my brand and strategies. Helping make things more self-service and templates that are part of my overall brand. That way I can hold more clients without hiring. I didn't have the passion to create an agency or consulting practice with "mini-me's." I was also exhausted running teams and was excited to be responsible for just me and the business.

These are tips on how to manage your career as a freelancer.

Pick Your Niche/Specialty

To be a successful freelancer, you need to niche down. Whatever field you are in, whether you are an artist, writer, computer programmer, chef, web designer, specialization is the key to differentiating yourself from the competition. Sometimes you may take a less-than-ideal assignment because you need the money, and that's fine. But keep your focus on how you can be in a position to continue to pick the next assignment based on your niche.

To find your niche:

1. Go back to your core competencies and list specific tasks you like to do in the area of your interest and expertise. Then create a job description, based on those tasks, and see if there is a market need for those tasks.

2. Make a list of clients in your niche you would like to work with. Try to talk to them if possible, to test how they value your skills. You can also take the first few opportunities to see if this is what you really would like to do. If not, then that is information for you to use in changing course.

3. Think through your value proposition and the way you'll package your products/services. When I asked Erica about this, she stressed having an open mind. *"Don't be afraid to adapt slightly if your product/market fit changes to be a bit different than you thought it would be."*

Find the Right Mentors and Champions

Find good mentors to bounce ideas off of and absorb as much advice as possible. Of course, we have revisited this topic as it pertains to so many areas of reinvesting in yourself. When I asked Erica about how she looked for mentors when she was starting out, she advised, "*Invest in yourself when it comes to your brand and your value proposition. I paid an expert to work on that before I even got started so I could be crystal clear on the value I was bringing to the market and my elevator pitch was tight.*"

Ways to Freelance

Work with a staffing agency

This is a great way to start out because when you work with a staffing agency or consulting company that can market you to their clients you can gain valuable experience for your resume and portfolio website. These agencies provide benefits like established client accounts and a structured pay system where you don't have to deal with the hassle of getting paid. The only downside is paying a commission on your jobs to the agency while you are working through them. If you are interested in full-time work, staffing agencies are a great option as temporary gigs sometimes turn into full-time work opportunities.

Independent contractor

If you go this route, you can register your own business or work directly as a 1099 contractor. Refer to the entrepreneurship chapter if you plan to go this path. Generally, independent contractors work with their network of partners or other resources to increase their own bandwidth. For example, if you are a general contractor, then you may want to know where to hire people to help you with projects and pay them by the job instead of putting them on your payroll. This is the best option if you want to eliminate the agency and platform fees. It requires a lot of networking and branding to continuously market yourself.

Erica Kuhl cites the seventeen years of experience she got at her previous company as a community-building leader as the key to her success. Because of her connections and her reputation, she started getting clients as soon as she launched her business.

Talent Platforms Also Known as Human Clouds

These platforms have really opened up the possibility of freelancing for millions of people. Of course, there is a lot of competition out there. It helps if you are well-rated on a platform, and that will happen if clients are happy with your work and leave good feedback that shows up on your profile.

The challenge with these cloud platforms is to continually market yourself. You can distinguish yourself by having excellent communication with the client and linking any work you have, including your own portfolio website, to your profile. If you can legitimize your fee and demonstrate results, you can convince people of the return on their investment when they hire you.

Testimonials on your site will go a long way toward this. For every job posted, there are a huge number of applicants, which makes the job of finding the right talent difficult for clients. The more ways you can find to make your profile stand out and the more experience under your belt, the easier it will be for you to start to distinguish yourself. Note that you will generally pay a 15–20% commission on these platforms for any work you do there.

Salaried employees of consulting firms on consulting engagements with clients

This is the most commonly misunderstood workforce of contingent workers. Most of the work is done under projects or what is referred to as a statement of work (SOW). Even though they are salaried employees, they are working for the company's clients.

Manage Your Finances

It's always wise to plan for ups and downs in your work. Barry Asin cautions, "*It's quite hard to be an instant success in freelancing unless you already have clients ready to give you business.*" This is why many people start out with a side hustle before they commit fully to this path.

It's a good rule of thumb to have at least six to twelve months of expenses set aside to give you the time to establish yourself as a freelancer. This is especially hard if you are on this path because you don't have any other choice. In this case, the first logical thing to do is to cut down on all the expenses that are not necessary.

To calculate monthly expenses, take an average of twenty-four months of expenditures. If you have not been able to keep track of your expenses, start now. Use this Google sheet to work on your finances or, if you prefer to use something you are familiar with, that's fine. Use money-management software that can help you give visibility and clarity regarding what you are spending.

I have found it's helpful to put spending into perspective using these three categories.

- Survive – mortgage or rent, food, clothes, education, utility bills, your hobbies that you can afford, family needs
- Live comfortably – occasionally going out to have fun, buy some stuff, donate, and help others, small getaways, any other entertainment, modest savings, etc.
- Thrive – go on lavish vacations, spend money on things that you like to do

By doing the above exercise, you will not only have your financial clarity but also a basis to determine how much you have to earn to move from surviving to thriving.

You should consider opening a separate business bank account to clearly separate business and personal finances.

Set aside money for taxes depending on your tax bracket, which can be 25–30%. If possible, try to find an interest-paying account where you can deposit tax money and pretend that money never existed. You also should pay quarterly taxes so that you do not get any surprises come April 15th.

If you find you have a cushion in the bank, then pay yourself first (10–20%) to develop saving habits. Put that money in another interest-bearing savings account or invest it and do not even think about spending that money. This will be your cushion for days when there is not enough work.

If you do hire an accountant, he or she will have experience in write-offs for self-employed individuals, including writing off a portion of your rent if you work at home.

Health insurance can prove to be one of your biggest expenses as a freelance worker. In the U.S., depending on the state you live in, there are multiple coverage options under the Affordable Care Act insurance exchanges. Also, there are sites like Freelancers Union that make things easier by handpicking health insurance plans for freelancers.[48]

That being said, this expense can be extremely prohibitive for freelancers who are just starting out. Health insurance has been a political football tossed around for decades, and there are no easy solutions. As Barry Asin pointed out,

One of the main reasons people want to work in a traditional full-time job in the US is because of health care. And to the extent that health

---

[48] https://www.freelancersunion.org/health/

care is coupled with employment, it encourages people to stay in jobs that they really don't want. And what we've seen over in Europe, where health care and employment are totally separated, we see significantly higher usage of temporary work, because there are more people who are willing to take temporary jobs if they don't have to worry about it, from a healthcare standpoint.

How to Set Your Prices

Determining your pricing involves several factors: your skill level, your reputation, what the typical going rate is, and what the clients are willing to pay. Rather than reinvent the wheel every time, create a repeatable pricing package based on the market rate and your unique niche.

It is quite tempting to take any rate you can get when you're establishing yourself in the beginning, and there is nothing wrong with that. But honor the value you bring, and once you have some credentials and samples, charge what you are worth. When you charge what you're worth, it builds your confidence and motivates you to do the job and give it your all. As you continue to do more freelancing, start experimenting by increasing your rates after every project and see what clients are willing to pay.

As a freelancer with a specialty, you might not be the right fit for many clients but there will be some clients for whom you are the perfect person for the job, and they will pay you the best price.

This is a formula that can help you come up with appropriate pricing for your services.

1. Determine your rough annual salary, assuming you were working full-time. If you are already working or recently left or got laid off, it is a good idea to use the recent salary as a starting point.

2. Increase that amount by approximately 30% to cover the additional expenses you will incur. Additionally, factor in your healthcare costs and potential additional taxes. According to TurboTax,[49] "America's self-employed must contend with a unique burden every April 15 (this year, April 17): the self-employment tax.[50] In addition to federal, state, and local income taxes, simply *being* self-employed subjects one to a separate 15.3% tax covering Social Security and Medicare. While W-2 employees "split" this rate with their employers, the IRS views an entrepreneur as both the employee *and* the employer. Thus, the higher tax rate." Of course, there are ways to lessen the impact of this additional tax by doing things like forming an S corp, deducting valid business expenses, etc.

3. In order to calculate the final billing rate based on the above steps, determine how many hours a year you would work at a traditional job. Because there is no sick pay or vacation pay, keep in mind you will either need to work more than the standard 2,080 hours (full-time employment hours).

4. A good rule of thumb is to double up your billing rate as compared to what you were getting paid as an annual salary. If you were making $75,000 per year in annual salary, the hourly rate, assuming 2,080 hours, works out to $36/hr. This means you need to bill at $70/hr if possible. If it is not possible to get this rate right out of the gate, keep that number in mind as something to work toward.

---

49 https://blog.turbotax.intuit.com/tax-tips/6-ways-to-pay-as-little-self-employment-tax-as-legally-necessary-3259/

50 http://www.irs.gov/businesses/small/article/0,,id=98846,00.html

Establishing Yourself

You want to legitimize your credentials, and the best way to do this is with experience, reviews, and links to your work. When you are first getting established, you may consider doing a few jobs for free to beef up your portfolio. If you are a graphic designer, ask your favorite restaurant if you can create a menu for them. If you are a writer, ask your lawyer or accountant if you can write a blog for them. This will be a great link and if their site is well established it is highly legitimizing, especially if you have a byline.

Rebecca submitted an essay to a dating column in the Los Angeles Times, and when her essay was published there, that instantly put her on the map. In a sea of freelancers online, this credential was game-changing for her writing career.

Communication Skills

Warren Buffet's advice about communication is spot on. He said that one easy way to become worth fifty percent more than you are now, is to hone your communication skills. You have to use your people skills to become a valuable part of the team, even if you are hired as a temporary worker. Soft skills are a huge differentiating factor for freelancers.

One way to communicate well with your clients is to have a response time limit policy. Establish definitive parameters for when agreements are signed, when work is due, how many deliverables/rewrites/polishes/revisions, etc. will be expected, and when. If there are milestones for payment, spell that out. If you don't work on weekends, state that in your contract. Being clear, professional, and reliable, goes a long way toward establishing boundaries and trustworthiness and it helps keep everyone on the same page, which will avoid misunderstandings.

Ivica Jandrijević has been quite successful freelancing. His book designs caught my attention, and though he was definitely not the cheapest, his samples and profile stood out in the piles of resumes and portfolios because of his talent and professionalism.

When I asked Ivica for his tips on finding success as a freelancer, this was his advice:

- *Honest communication. Never lie to your clients. Be true to your work, yourself, and your clients.*

- *Treat people well when you're on a job. More doors will open just by being nice. If you work with difficult personalities, remember not to take mood swings and cutting comments personally. Every situation is a learning experience. Stand by your work and always be open to tweaking it per client suggestion.*

- *Be open about what you're looking for regarding the work environment, compensation, and the actual work itself. Everyone should be on the same page to avoid any unexpected confusion or frustration.*

Customers as Your Evangelists

Reviews and testimonials go a long way to establishing any business, and when you are a freelancer starting out, they are critical. The best testimonials speak to an objective or a reservation the client had and explain that she not only ended up seeing the value in your work but at the end of the day wound up with an excellent return on her investment. This is golden for your business because other clients will relate and feel convinced to give you a try when they see that you've earned an impressive reputation.

If you are starting out, then you may not have customers to give testimonials yet. In that case, ask colleagues, professors, or friends to talk about your talent and work ethic. LinkedIn is a great platform for endorsements.

There are several ways you can incentivize your customers to give good reviews and referrals. My suggestion is to focus on doing a great job and let the work speak for itself. Sometimes you can offer a bonus—going an extra mile for them in exchange for a testimonial. Repurpose your testimonials using them on every platform to spread the good word.

If you work on a platform like Upwork and a client randomly left negative feedback, there are ways of getting it removed if you can prove that it is not legitimate.

Take Your Work, and Yourself, Seriously

While having no boss gives you the freedom to set your own hours, it also gives you the freedom to lose track of time. Habits are the key to working for yourself. Your habits influence your behaviors, which establish your outcomes, which will determine the success of your business. These are tips for establishing good work habits:

Set boundaries

If you can work at home, that's great, because obviously, it saves on overhead. However, if you have a hard time convincing your family/housemates that you are working and you are unavailable, you will have to figure out how to establish boundaries.

When I asked Ivica about lessons he had learned and things he might do differently if he were to start over again, he said: *"I would start with finding an office. I would not work at home for two years. It has its benefits, but it has its downsides also."*

If you need to get in your zone and get away from home but can't afford an office, check out apps that allow you to use communal workspaces on a subscription basis. You can input your zip code and pull up an office that is nearby. These apps are a great asset for a very reasonable price. Libraries are also an option for getting in a productive zone. They usually have private rooms you can sign up for to work undisturbed for a block of time.

Remove distractions

You may not realize how distracted you are, but if you are someone who enjoys social media, it's quite possible you are wasting several hours a week on various apps and sites. Focus on your goals and remember that FOMO can be the death of productivity!

For tempting smartphones, there are any number of tricks you can do to make your phone look and seem less attractive. You can have a greyed out, nondescript home screen, remove social media apps, and definitely silence alerts, setting your phone to DND (with the exception of immediate family or friends who you want to allow).

Set routines

I'm not going to tell you when you should work—some people are night owls, and some people, like myself, will wake at 3:30 a.m. to work, partly because my team is in India. Some find that the scene is important—the music, lighting, ritual pen/prop — whatever it is. Get into your productive zone at some point during the day and repeat the next day, (and the next).

Compartmentalize

If you have five different gigs one week, it's challenging to continually take off one hat and put on another. Try to work in blocks where you can focus on one job and maybe even do the whole thing in one or two days, then move on to the next. When you flit between client assignments you can lose traction/momentum and find yourself re-reading client briefs to refamiliarize yourself with the requirements over and over again. It's frustrating to feel like you're starting all over again and it's not a good use of your time.

Focus

The Pomodoro Technique has gained popularity in the last few years. This method was invented in the early 1990s by entrepreneur and author Francesco Cirillo. Cirillo named the system "Pomodoro" after the tomato-shaped timer he used to track his work as a university student.

I think it's such a useful technique because it's a way to work in bite-size segments. Rather than getting overwhelmed by the task ahead of you, when you use the Pomodoro Method you set a timer for twenty-five or thirty minutes, work straight through, and take a break when the timer goes off. When you stack three or four Pomodoro sessions together you've already got a solid morning of work behind you. It's great for your brain and your body to get some breaks when you move around, even for a moment, and removing your eyes from the screen, or phone or page for a rest helps a lot. Knowing you have built-in breaks and you're allowing yourself a breather helps with stress levels too.

Your Branding Assets

Refer to the branding chapter for the importance of creating a personal brand. Many freelancers make the mistake of simply creating a site-specific profile for whatever platform they're working on, but your own website is the most important calling card you have. Your work lives there, as well as your bio, testimonials, case studies, and any awards or press mention you have received.

It's easy to get caught up in social media and forget about managing your own assets like your website where you can showcase your expertise. Don't let this happen and instead prioritize maintaining your website and most importantly, creating and optimizing content for SEO. For example, consistently publishing blog posts that are SEO-optimized allows you to target multiple keywords — potential client search queries — so you can consistently drive traffic and leads to your site.

Marketing and Sales

When you work for yourself, you are a commodity, and you must market yourself. 2020 was a painful wake-up call for anyone who has not put an effort into online marketing. When something like a global pandemic happens and you can only reach customers online, your site had better be optimized for visibility, easily searchable on Google and your value proposition for potential clients should be very clear.

You may choose to hire a digital marketing specialist to either do regular or intermittent work to optimize your site. You can also look into software to help you with marketing your services or products.

Facebook ads allow you to target a specific niche, so you may want to consider a budget for these internet ads that generally don't cost that much.

Expanding Your Horizons

If you become successful, then very soon you may end up getting more work than you are able to handle on your own. Plan on this happening and think about how you will build your own teams of freelancers who you can trust to do quality work that you would be comfortable having your name on.

Optimization and Outsourcing

Several freelancers find themselves drowning in emails and spreadsheets and end up doing tasks that do not come naturally to them. This is what I call falling into a productivity black hole. You will lose time doing things like tracking invoicing and you will make mistakes, such as sending the wrong invoice or forgetting to bill the clients altogether.

Before you get too overwhelmed, remember, software is your friend! You can find excellent productivity software for managing a lot of these tasks.

For every task that is not your strong suit, decide whether it can be automated or outsourced. I asked Erica how she navigated this terrain when she was setting up her freelance business.

I invest in experts for my taxes and accounting since it's more complicated than in days past running my own business. I also invest in design because branding is so important. My website is the main source of traffic and I wanted it to be amazing, so I worked with experts on building and designing that aspect. I look for work to outsource that is not directly associated with client facing work. For example, doing competitive analysis is something that can be done behind the scenes without deep understanding of the client.

Because things are evolving every day and more and more people are experiencing job uncertainty, everyone should think like a gig worker and be ready to pivot. It can be a very rewarding job, but clearly not without its complexities. When I asked Erica if she had any regrets about becoming a one-woman army, she replied:

Not for one second. I'm so much happier, I feel valued, and I feel like I'm using the skills I worked so hard to build for good. I love being my own boss and I drive myself pretty hard, but I still make it a priority to protect spots that are for me and my lifestyle. I am nearly 99.9% certain I'll never go back to a traditional job—at least full-time. I am having too much fun working for all these amazing companies and building amazing community experiences for them.

* * * *

At this point, you have figured out that success or failure in this path is 100% dependent on you. If you do the research and position yourself with the right mindset and the right tools, freelancing can help you build a sustainable business. Take the time to do things properly and set yourself up for a career that is both gratifying and financially rewarding.

Time to Gear up to Be Accountable for Your Success

1. Think about your area of expertise and how you can niche down. Canvas friends, family, mentors, and potential customers to see if they see the value in your offer. Would they buy services/products from you?

2. Dip your toe in the water with a side hustle, or a post on a human cloud site. Do a search as someone looking for talent so you can see what your competition on the platform is charging. Check out their profiles to see which ones get a lot of hits.

3. Build up testimonials on your site or your profile. If you don't have any, do a job for an acquaintance—give them a great price—and have them review your work so you have a testimonial to build on.

YOUR CANVAS

IN THE INTRODUCTION of this book, I talked about creating a cutting-edge, practical toolkit which is the Tri-R Canvas—a visual chart with elements you will fill in using the thought-provoking, hands-on questions from each chapter that will help you to articulate your experience.

The Tri-R canvas is based around the concept of the business model lean canvas. The business model canvas is a strategic management tool that lets you visualize and assess your business idea or concept. It's a one-page document containing nine boxes that represent different fundamental elements of a business.

Using this structure, I have expanded the purpose to fit your life, rather than just your business. The beauty and simplicity of the model compels you to distill your thoughts into concise, actionable statements. By doing so, you will achieve clarity on what you want. Now it's time to put together your canvas that will serve as a blueprint to inspire and motivate you going forward in whatever career path you choose for achieving a successful, happy, and harmonious life.

Please download the online version of the canvas at Tri-R Canvas[51] or create a copy of it so you can work in the document.

Fill in the following blocks using **only bullet points not exceeding 3–5 points** in each block. Give yourself a timeframe for the desired outcome. Be thoughtful and give yourself realistic goals, but don't be afraid to take risks and step outside your comfort zone. It will only be possible if you give yourself 100% commitment.

Timeframe: start date, end date

_____

_____

1. How do you want your story to unfold?

_____

_____

_____

_____

_____

---

[51] https://docs.google.com/document/d/1vbTt3FhP3ScTGDzm-gptI0a9gBNfu0KYacCesqKI5NA/edit

2. Your happiness list, realistic and achievable in the timeframe you give yourself.

_____

_____

_____

_____

_____

3. Core Competencies—what's your brand?

_____

_____

_____

_____

_____

4. Mentors, support net

_____

_____

_____

_____

5. Your ecosystem and network

_____

_____

6. Your path forward – actions and steps

7. Finances – analysis and goals

8. Wellness goals

9. Friends and family – check in

_____
_____
_____
_____
_____
_____

BMS rating and happiness score

_____
_____
_____
_____
_____
_____

Now put all this content in the one-page document shown below. Print this document and display it where you can see it on a daily basis. Also share this document with your mentors, friends, and family and request them to make you accountable for your goals. Boldly share your desires and also how you are achieving them. Ask anyone and everyone who can help to give direction and motivation. Join our Career Interrupted community where you can meet like-minded people and form a core group who can continue to cheer your progress and guide you on the path to work-life harmony.

Your Canvas

Start Date:

End Date:

Your Story	What makes you happy	Financial Goals	Mentors, Support Net	Career – Next Steps
	Core Competencies		Ecosystem, Network	
Wellness Goals			Friends and Family	

BMS Rating and Happiness Score

EPILOGUE

IF YOU GET to the end of this book and you are surprised that it was not a typical career guidebook, I hope you have a smile on your face at that realization! I could not have written a substantive career guide without having you take a deep dive to look at who you are, what you envision for your career, and how you personally hope to achieve work-life harmony. If you find that *Career Interrupted* and the workbook and canvas you created become your personalized blueprint for a balanced three-legged stool, I will know that the book is a success.

My last piece of advice is, please don't stop growing and learning. Although you have come to the end of the book, I hope that it is just a beginning for you as you reassess your career trajectory and forge the path ahead. Keep the momentum going, keep branching out, keep journaling your dreams and hopes, and continue to enhance your personal and professional networking efforts.

As for Rebecca and me, this was a tremendously enriching experience. The theme of "a rising tide lifts all boats" was instilled in me from birth, growing up in a communal household with my immediate family as well as aunts, uncles, and a dozen cousins who are all dear to me. We were there to share in each other's joys and heartaches, we taught each other and learned from each other every day.

In creating a book to guide you on your journey, I had no idea how much I would learn along the way about getting in touch with my own emotions. The power of writing all of this down was incredible. It also opened up my awareness of different peoples' experiences. As we researched and wrote, I doubled down on my belief in showcasing your talents and being bold. I got turned on to this lifelong learning path which I have begun to seek out, taking online courses, reading numerous books to have a greater understanding of the subjects we were writing about, and I have made a point to drink my own medicine and prioritize my own physical wellness. In the writing of the book, I started having open conversations with family and laughing with them more.

As for Rebecca, one small tip she took was customizing her LinkedIn URL. On a deeper level, she realized that having a book like this when she was returning to work after a career break would have been life-changing. She came at the writing and research from an angle of wanting to boost confidence and expose opportunities for anyone returning to work, laid off, or simply burned out and feeling out of balance for whatever reason. More than anything, Rebecca was touched by all the people in her life that were willing to mentor her in reinvesting in herself as she transitioned from a screenwriting background to marketing and book writing. Most of the people we reached out to for interviews for the book were happy to help. It's very true that through teaching you learn, and it has been a very gratifying experience for both of us.

We hope that this book helps you as much as it helped us. If it does, please gift the book to your friends and family to help them through their career crossroads.

If you want to keep learning, we would love to have you join our community on our website. Let's keep an open dialogue and welcome anyone who could use a little encouragement. Let's listen to each other, support each other, add onto ideas sparked from the book, and walk the walk when it comes to networking! Apart from building on the teachings of this book, our workshops are a place to further connections, share leads, share frustrations, ask for help, or offer a different perspective on what one of your peers is going through. If someone you care about is at a career crossroads, pick up a copy of the book for them and tell them that when one door closes, another one opens.

Lastly, I just want to add to the self-care discussion and stress (no pun intended) how important it is to not be too hard on yourself. If you are feeling frustrated that you have yet to hit your career goals, take the long view. Life is long, nothing is set in stone, and if you act with intention, you can realize anything you set your mind to achieve.

And remember, Rome was not built in a day. If you take small steps every day toward your goal, congratulate yourself for being determined, and take pride in every victory, no matter how small. The choices we make determine our destiny, and you should know that you have everything within you that you need to steer your ship to catch the wind and sail.

ACKNOWLEDGMENTS

Writing acknowledgements fills me with gratitude and I'm finding it so difficult to pick names to thank. This book is a result of all the life experiences, people who have influenced me directly and indirectly. Every moment of writing this book from the time of ideation to finally completing it, was full of fun and learning.

I am so grateful for everyone who has helped shape this book. Our book village consists of 1 author, 1 supporting author, 44 contributors, 1 book designer, 1 developmental editor, 1 copy editor, 1 illustrator, and 1 very important champion/critic, Ritika Gupta. It is the collective wisdom and efforts of everyone that create this relevant and authentic guide for every reader going through their career crossroads.

I will start by thanking my amazing writing buddy, who I call my soul sister, Rebecca, for not only helping express my words and thoughts so beautifully but also brainstorming with me on the direction of this book. Thanks Rebecca, this is the start of our journey to many more books together.

Our whole book team, Ingrid Emerick, Ivica Jandrijević, Elena Brighittini, Dan Crissman, and Chad Robertson not only worked to meet deadlines but also gave excellent creative suggestions.

I would especially like to thank my daughter, Ritika Gupta, wise beyond her fourteen years, who has been my support not only emotionally but also as a contributor. Her intuitive editing skills really shone as she doggedly kept me on point, reminding me to cut down all my anecdotes and focus on always helping the reader. She helped me break through my writer's block, making me ginger-masala tea and massaging my back as I sat at my computer. She was there to cheer me up when I was running behind, missing deadlines that I had set for the book. She somehow had the wisdom to know that taking my time and doing it right was more important than doing it quickly.

For my son, Rohan, whose intellect, entrepreneurial passion, peer wisdom(peersdom) and dancing skills raise my wellness quotient every day. I appreciate both of these kids for picking up the slack, cooking and cleaning on the days when I locked myself in my office to work on this manuscript.

For my husband Rajeev, for insisting on leaving me alone and giving me space to devote myself to this project, but at the same time always being there in the background to buoy my spirits, encourage me, and share his thoughts and smart insights on anything I was stuck on.

For my mom in India whose love and support is always there, no matter the distance. I have tried, in my own life, to follow in her footsteps as a loving, doting parent, while at the same time pursuing my passions in a professional career—an option that was not available to her in those days.

Thanks to my dad, Narmdeshwar Nath Gupta, who is no longer with us in person but regardless, I feel his presence and support in everything I do. He embodied kindness, encouragement, and love, and taught me the true meaning of life by always smiling and helping bring a smile to others' faces.

Many thanks to my elder brother Sunil Gupta, who has always showered his unconditional love and support. He funded my college education for MCA which helped me build a career in the IT industry. He has been the solid pillar of our family, taking care of everyone's emotions and needs.

And my brother Niraj Gupta, 2 years older than me, who was more like a friend when we were growing up. He taught me all the life skills: reading, writing, making tea, biking, sewing, and also having fun. I still remember the incident when my long flowing hair got stuck in the hair dryer and he was the one who took several hours to gently remove the strands of hair, one at a time, so I would not have to cut it.

My nephew, Priyanshu, who helped review the manuscript, which encouraged him to do some soul searching and use strategies while paving his own career path.

To my sister-in-law, Promila Kumar, for showing me the path for a woman to have both family and a career without having to choose one over the other. I still remember staying with her for a few days right after my wedding and having an opportunity to learn firsthand how, with the right time management skills and will power, it can be done so easily and seamlessly.

To my many relatives in India, though I don't get to see you nearly enough, you are always here with me in spirit. I am who I am today because of your love, friendship, and guidance. I learned the value of social wellbeing and emotional intelligence by being part of such a big and loving family who are there to support each other.

To all the incredible mentors, teachers, advisors, and friends in my personal and professional circle; it took that village to get me here.

And last but not least, my fur baby, Rocky, for always being there to cuddle and bring energy whenever I felt a bit down.

~ **Reena Gupta**

I would like to echo Reena's sentiments of gratitude for our book village. Who knew that from a random LinkedIn message I would find my partner, Reena, who would help me begin an exciting new professional chapter of my life. While on lockdown, we Zoomed every day for four months, and when we finally got to meet in person in LA, I felt it was just the beginning of a lifelong friendship and partnership.

I am amazed every day by the love, creativity, and talent of my boys, Aidan, and Beckett, who are coming into their own as young men going off into the world. I could not be more proud of both of them. They have been my "why" for the last twenty-two years, and now that I am reconnecting with my professional passion, writing, they are there in my corner cheering for me. I am inspired by them every day—they are that corny "wind beneath my wings," always!

Thank you to Daniel Landau for being my sounding board, editing pages over green tea with me at Cafe Bolivar. A special thanks to David Callahan. We were skateboarding buddies and best friends at age ten, and now all these years later David has been an unwavering mentor and support at a challenging time in my life. Thank you for helping me reinvent and reinvest in myself.

They say you can't choose your family, but if I could I wouldn't change a thing. Thank you to my dad, Maurice. I lost him when I was turning thirty, but he is always with me cheering my every success, no matter how big or small. If he were here today he would still be asking, "*How ya doing kid?*" and reminding me to watch my crossing.

Thanks to my sisters Madeleine and Lisa for their love and encouragement, and for picking up the pieces of me when I fall apart. I love our sister trips! Thanks, Mom, for being a badass feminist who took us to march on Washington for the Equal Rights Amendment in the '70s and for inspiring me with your love and support. You are an amazing woman and my blueprint for happiness, success, and work-life harmony.

Thank you to my cousin Joan Torres who has inspired me with her celebrated writing success and most of all for remaining my biggest champion ever since she read the first short story I wrote.

To the incredible and lovely women I get to call my best friends—you bring the warm and fuzzy and you have extended my life with all the love, laughter, plantains, and margaritas.

Last, but certainly not least, I would like to thank my partner Neil, who has been my North Star and my rock all at once. We bonded over Led Zeppelin and being transplanted New Yorkers in the City of Angels. Thank you for sheltering in place with me and putting up with my Oscar Madison tendencies.

~ **Rebecca Cullen**

Made in the USA
Middletown, DE
15 September 2021